PORTRAIT OF A UNIVERSITY
1851–1951

JOHN OWENS

From a Medallion by T. Woolner

[*Frontispiece*

PORTRAIT
OF A
UNIVERSITY
1851—1951

TO COMMEMORATE THE CENTENARY OF
MANCHESTER UNIVERSITY

BY

H. B. CHARLTON, M.A., Litt.D.

*Professor of English Literature, Honorary Doctor
of the Universities of Leeds
and Dijon*

MANCHESTER UNIVERSITY PRESS

Published by the University of Manchester
at the University Press
8-10 Wright Street
Manchester, 15
1951

CONTENTS

PAGE

FOREWORD. *By Sir John Stopford, M.D., Sc.D., F.R.C.P., F.R.S., Vice-Chancellor* ix

CHAP.

I. THE OCCASION 1

II. THE PREPARATION 13

III. THE FOUNDATION 22

IV. COLLEGE TO UNIVERSITY: THE ROSCOE-WARD EPOCH . . 53

V. FEDERAL TO FREE UNIVERSITY: THE SCHUSTER-TOUT EPOCH . 78

VI. THE ALEXANDER VERSION OF THE MANCHESTER IDEA . . 97

VII. MANCHESTER UNIVERSITY: IDEA INTO REALITY . . . 110

APPENDICES:

I. *Chronological* 138

II. *Officers: (A) Owens College before the Victoria University of Manchester (1903); (B) Offices created by the formation of the (Federal) Victoria University (1880); (C) Victoria University of Manchester (1903)* 139

III. *Financial Resources of the University: (A) Benefactions; (B) Income* 143

IV. *Admission of Women to University Status* . . . 153

V. *Student Numbers* 164

VI. *Physical Expansion: Extensions of Site, and Erection of New Buildings* 168

VII. *Professors and Members of Senate, 1851–1951* . . . 172

VIII. *Staff Numbers* 183

LIST OF ILLUSTRATIONS

(a) PORTRAITS

FACING
PAGE

JOHN OWENS (*medallion by T. Woolner*) . . . *Frontispiece*

THE SENATE, 1862–1863 16

THE SENATE, 1872–1873 17

A. J. SCOTT, PRINCIPAL 1851–1857 26

J. G. GREENWOOD, PRINCIPAL 1857–1889 30

A. W. WARD, PRINCIPAL 1889–1897 42

ALFRED HOPKINSON, PRINCIPAL 1898–1904, VICE-CHANCELLOR OF MAN-
CHESTER UNIVERSITY, 1904–1913 54

THE SENATE, 1900 62

THE SENATE, 1944 63

F. E. WEISS, VICE-CHANCELLOR 1913–1915 82

SIR HENRY A. MIERS, VICE-CHANCELLOR 1915–1926 . . . 90

SIR WALTER H. MOBERLY, VICE-CHANCELLOR 1926–1934 . . 98

SIR JOHN STOPFORD, VICE-CHANCELLOR 1934– 112

LORD SIMON OF WYTHENSHAWE, CHAIRMAN OF COUNCIL, 1941– . 122

LORD WOOLTON, CHANCELLOR OF THE UNIVERSITY, 1944– . . 134

(b) VIEWS

OWENS COLLEGE, QUAY STREET 4

SKETCH OF THE MAIN BUILDING AND THE MUSEUM, 1894 . . 4

OWENS COLLEGE, *circa* 1876 5

THE QUADRANGLE, *circa* 1880 5

THE QUADRANGLE, *circa* 1890 74

ETCHING OF THE OXFORD ROAD FRONTAGE, *circa* 1926 . . 74

THE OXFORD ROAD FRONTAGE WITH THE WHITWORTH HALL, 1902 . 75

vii

	FACING PAGE
THE COLLEGE OF TECHNOLOGY, *circa* 1905	86
TWO VIEWS OF ASHBURNE HALL	106
THE ARTS LIBRARY, 1937	107
THE TURNER DENTAL SCHOOL, 1940	107
THE ARTS BUILDING, 1919	154
THE WHITWORTH HALL (INTERIOR)	162

(c) PLANS

THE UNIVERSITY IN 1888	*page* 170
,, ,, 1911	,, 171
,, ,, 1950	*Folding Plate* ,, 172

FOREWORD

by

SIR JOHN STOPFORD, M.D., Sc.D., F.R.C.P., F.R.S., *Vice-Chancellor*

VERY wisely, in my opinion, Professor Charlton has not written a history of the past hundred years ; instead he has set himself a more difficult task and has achieved his object admirably. With his pen he has sketched a portrait of a new form of university which stimulated a great educational movement and provided the pattern for others.

John Owens believed that social progress was to be secured through education and in a few plain words he stated the ideal of what he would like a College to be. Professor Charlton traces the evolution of that ideal and describes in a most fascinating and convincing fashion how it inspired a series of remarkable men, who seized this unique opportunity to influence fundamentally academic education in this country. These men realised that they inherited a great mission and they possessed a faith and a devotion to the cause which has meant so much to Owens College and the University. The reader will appreciate how exceptionally fortunate Manchester was to have and to hold laymen and teachers who made educational history and had the courage and imagination to foster an ideal. Professor Charlton tells us about these men, develops his portrait with great skill and manifests a penetrating understanding of the spirit which prompted so many of the builders of the University.

It is well known that Owens College performed a unique pioneering experiment and made the path easier for others, but Professor Charlton has enabled us to see more clearly than ever before how the original motive has persisted down the century and how it has been interpreted in the ever-changing environment. No one previously has been able to discover so definitely the central thread which continues unbroken down the hundred years and which, he maintains, continues to guide us. He advances cogent evidence which leads him to believe that the university to-day is still propelled by the original ideal and is still essentially faithful to the primary purpose of its Founder.

Professor Charlton has rendered outstanding service to the university of Manchester since his first appointment thirty-nine years ago when he left the sister university of Leeds. We are now placed even more in his debt by the publication of this centenary volume and I desire to congratulate him as well as thank him for what he has achieved. He writes from intimate knowledge of a number of the people he mentions ; he has made an exhaustive study of the documents ; he possesses an unshakable belief in the ideal which he describes and he presents his findings in his own inimitable style. The members of Council and Senate were convinced that he was the person to undertake this formidable and important service and the pages which follow prove how right was that decision and how successful he has been. In my opinion he has made a notable and impressive contribution which will prove of real value to all interested in higher education.

CHAPTER I

THE OCCASION

A T a meeting of the Senate of the University on 16th January, 1947, the Vice-Chancellor drew attention to the fact that the centenary of Owens College, the academic foundation from which the University of Manchester grew, would fall in 1951. He announced that he proposed shortly to ask the Council of the University to appoint an appropriate committee to consider plans for the Centenary celebration. Council forthwith set up a joint-committee of Council and Senate, and from time to time, as it became expedient, it has added other members. But, in a university which seventy years earlier Roscoe had called " the University of the Busy ", 1947 was a year which left little respite from the vastly increased burden of accommodating and teaching almost twice as many students as in 1939. Hence it was not until April 1948 that a sub-committee, of which I was chairman, met to consider whether any commemorative volume should be prepared for the occasion, and if so, what sort of a volume it should be. The sub-committee reported that in the short period available, which was no more than what leisure time could be found in two summer vacations, it would be impossible to contemplate the preparation of a worthy and adequate history of the foundation during its first hundred years of life. It recommended, however, that an attempt might be made to provide a volume which should seek to present, not a history, but a kind of survey in outline of the University, with sketches of its shape and function at the more significant stages of its growth from infancy to adolescence, from adolescence to manhood, and from manhood to full maturity. For, like a human being, Manchester University is a distinctive organism ; and like human beings, it has its biography. As with human beings, too, its character and personality are a complex autonomy on which ancestry, immediate parentage, the prevailing pressure of its physical, moral, social and religious environment, and all other factors which comprise its ecology in time and place, have exerted their shaping energies. Manchester University has grown in a natural way to its own distinctive nature. It began with roots deep in the soil of its home. It was nourished by its intellectual environment. The climate of Manchester opinion, not only on affairs of industry and commerce, but on issues of politics, morals and religion, was never more invigorating and creative than in the mid-nineteenth century. The Manchester of 1850 was indeed a hive of pulsating industry. " Second town of the kingdom ", as Cobden had called it, a town of men immersed in the development of industry and commerce, it was yet a place in which an intellectual, an artistic and, above all, a moral culture was vigorously renewing itself. Even at the beginning of the century, de Quincey, who had lived in Manchester as a schoolboy without any fondness for it, on later acquaintance testified to the liveliness of its cultural interests : " in Manchester I have witnessed more interesting conversation, as much information, and more eloquence in conveying it, than is usual in literary cities or places professedly learned . . . the day given to business and active duties, the evening to relaxation . . . so that books are more cordially enjoyed ". In the 1840's Manchester was the home of Mrs. Gaskell, the Misses Jewsbury, and Miss Martineau. In 1840, the historian Froude, who had just married Charles Kingsley's sister, included Manchester in his wedding tour in order to meet the Gaskells and the Jewsburys. Moreover, one of the most active of Manchester's cultural activities was its unremitting effort to develop national education as the most potent instrument of a moral civilisation. It had already seen one of its leading citizens, a medical man, Dr. Kay, dedicate his career to the service of the Government in its earliest organisation for advising on elementary education : as Sir James Kay-Shuttleworth, he devoted his life as an educational official to working " for the claims of the civil power to control the education of the country ". The University is the child of the place, of the people and of the time : it is the academic incarnation of the genius of its city and of its province.

The picture of the University which the committee envisaged would have comprised a series of sketches depicting college and university at climacteric stages of their growth, when the forces inherent in them were realising and then fulfilling their own nature. For portraying such a spiritually organic process adequately, three qualifications are necessary ; first, an intimate familiarity with all material facts of the University's history; secondly, a biologist's insight for detecting the relationship between forms and functions; and thirdly, an artist's genius for discerning and transmitting the soul of his subject. Neither the committee nor its chairman, however, had realised the exact nature of the undertaking when they committed themselves to the volume. Moreover, as the chairman had himself suggested such a volume, they imposed the writing of it on him, that is, on me. Some excuse for their decision is that I am one of the few people still on the academic staff of the University who were appointed to it before the year (1914) to which the last historical account of the University extended. I owe to the committee and to the University some justification for my accepting the authorship, and even more, for my having greatly curtailed the first plan of the project. The change of plan is the easier to explain. Only when the work started did one begin to realise the enormity of the undertaking, and to recognise that even if one had had the necessary personal qualities to fulfil the task, the mere time factor would have prevented its realisation. It seemed better therefore to adopt a more restricted scope, if one could be found, which, though more restricted, might none the less seem an appropriate theme for a centenary volume. Manchester's was the first of the many Victorian colleges which later became the modern universities. It is no mere Manchester boast to claim that not only was Manchester first, but that Manchester's example, in general, set the pattern for the rest of the country. In its early days this was recognised officially by Her Majesty's Government : when in 1889, the Treasury gave its first grants to university colleges, it gave Owens College more than any other; in 1895, the Treasury's inspection committee (the equivalent of the modern University Grants Committee) reported that Manchester was strongest of the provincial colleges; four years later, the committee was impressed by the " combination of public spirit, business capacity and enthusiasm for learning which has made the college what it is ". What the tradition which Manchester was making was to mean in the whole pattern of British academic education was finely expressed by Sir Charles Grant Robertson, Vice-Chancellor of Birmingham University, in a letter (printed pp. 128–9 below) to the press on the occasion of Sir A. W. Ward's death in 1924. It seemed, therefore, that though an adequate historical survey of the University could not be written for the occasion, it might be possible to trace, and in tracing, to define the Manchester academic tradition. Hence, the theme of this volume is to follow the realisation of the academic and social purposes explicit and implicit in the minds of our Founder and of those of his friends to whom he entrusted the shaping of his foundation. The central thread is to follow a new educational concept fulfilling itself in response to emergent circumstance, to see the evolving idea of a new form of university, a university with a new conception of its place in and its duty to society.

So much for my alteration of the nature of the centenary volume which the committee authorised. But though it is not easy to justify my acceptance of the authorship of the volume, it is very easy to explain it. I have spent the whole of my adult life, that is, the last thirty-nine years of it, as lecturer and professor in Manchester University. As soon as I came to Manchester in 1912, I became a disciple of T. F. Tout and an ardent believer in his idea of our university. Indeed, I suspect that my election to the assistant lectureship in English Literature was mainly brought about by Tout, who was an old Balliol contemporary and close friend of my own teacher at Leeds University, C. E. Vaughan. In the formative years of our first experiences of teaching in Manchester University, it was meetings with Tout which made me and my contemporaries realise how vital and how unique was the opportunity of Manchester in shaping the form of the academic education of the country for the next century. Tout inspired a deep faith in the University, a faith which as early as 1908 he had publicly declared in these words : " my main point is, have confidence in the mission of the new University : pray accept what I have said as uttered in no spirit of glorification or boasting : it is the simple expression of faith in the ideal animating the new University which a life devoted to its service has inspired." Manchester has been fortunate in attracting to its service men like Tout who have made that service their life's work, or, at least, the work of their most creative years. In my own time in Manchester, Tout, Alexander, Dixon, Lamb, Herford, Conway, Tait, Fiddes, Peake and Lapworth were the inheritors of the tradition which had been passed on to them from Greenwood, Theodores, Osborne Reynolds, Roscoe, Morgan, Schorlemmer, Ward, Schuster, Perkin and Hopkinson. To come into such a community was an exhilarating experience. At times it could be a disconcerting one. Soon after my arrival, for instance, Fiddes, as was a regular habit of his, gave a dinner for a few of the elder statesmen and a few of the youngest newcomers. I found myself next to an eminent scientist. During soup, his first remark to me was " Had I ever climbed the Andes ? " I muttered " No." Well, he had. With the

OWENS COLLEGE, QUAY STREET
(From a sketch by W. E. Walker, 1874)

THE MAIN BUILDING AND THE MUSEUM, 1894
(From a sketch by H. E. Tidmarsh in "Manchester, Old and New", 1894)

OWENS COLLEGE, *circa* 1876
(*Photograph published in "Manchester as it is", 1878*)

THE QUADRANGLE, *circa* 1880

fish, he turned to me again : " Had I ever navigated a ship down the West Coast of Africa ? " Again, in awed humility, I could only say " No." But with the entrée, we found a common topic : we talked of Horace. Taking it all round, however, Manchester in those days was a happy initiation for the young new members of its staff. There were the Wednesday evenings, almost whenever one wanted, at Alexander's. At half-past eight he would bring his aged mother in on his arm, and lead her to the corner chair of honour ; at nine o'clock he would escort her back to her room, return, and offer whisky to his male guests. Or there was Unwin, whose mode of initiating the newcomers was to invite them to walk with him anywhere in the circle of a mile around the University. Every street, every house, almost every doorway, prompted remarks on them as illustrations of different phases or aspects in the historical growth of Manchester. One soon felt at home. Admitted to the community, moreover, one began to get glimpses, at first, of course, from afar, of the distinctive attributes of the older professors, and of their rôle in guiding the growth of the University. As one grew older oneself, one's view of the process was a closer one, and, in due time, one felt oneself to be really participating in it. One saw how much and how vitally the personality of the professor was the determining factor in the evolution of our academic policy. Unfortunately, it is impossible to depict here those shaping spirits. Up to twenty years ago one only knew them as youth knows age. Now, after another twenty years, when one has known them more intimately as colleagues, that is, when one has seen even more fully to what extent they were clarifying and enlarging the idea of Manchester University, one is still prevented from recording an assessment. For, happily, so many of them are still alive.

Had it not been for the war, our centenary would have been worthily commemorated in an authoritative historical volume. That volume, or series of volumes, must surely be written, and be written very soon, before the immense mass of widely disparate material available for it becomes unmanageable by its bulk or less accessible by its dispersion than it is at present. The achievements of the University in the hundred years of its life impose on it an obligation to secure an adequate record of itself. As Owens College, it began as a new educational and social experiment. It became the pioneer of a new kind of academic organisation. It has set a pattern which, in the coming hundred years, seems destined to be the most widely available type of university education in this country. In the meantime it has grown to its own maturity : a university within the walls of which both the Chancellor and the Vice-Chancellor were formerly undergraduates has surely attained ripeness. It has really earned a history of itself. Something towards that history has already been done. There are two comprehensive and substantial volumes which, between them, bring the story down to 1914, the first, by Joseph Thompson, recording it to 1886, and the second, by Edward Fiddes, carrying it to 1914.

Joseph Thompson was a typical representative of those Manchester men who saw how John Owens' foundation provided a means by which their spiritual and cultural ideals could be attained. Son and grandson of influential business men, and destined to carry on the family cotton-weaving business in the Ardwick mills, as a boy he was quickly transferred from school to industry : and his father's early death soon threw on him the whole burden of responsibility for the firm. Yet, though not until after his marriage, he resumed his formal education by enrolling in the classes at Owens College in its Quay Street days. Afterwards, as a fervent Liberal of the John Bright school and as a devout Congregationalist, he divided his time between business and public service. His main activities in public life were directed to the work of the city council and to the governing body of Owens College. To the well-being of the college he was unsparing in devotion. He was an early Trustee, a Life-Governor, Treasurer up to 1908, and from 1887 to 1904 he was Chairman of the college. He knew the place and all those closely connected with it from its infancy. His book *The Owens College, its Foundation and Growth* (Cornish, Manchester, 1886) with its 700 pages, has the stately expansiveness of Victorian biography. It is much more than a formal compilation of academic facts. Its detail is rich in the intimacies of personal acquaintance-ship. It allows one to see how the personalities of the trustees, the governors and the early teachers stamped themselves on their new creation.

Edward Fiddes's volume, *Chapters in the History of Owens College and of Manchester University 1851–1914* (Manchester University Press, 1937), is in a different mould. Fiddes had come to Manchester as an assistant lecturer in Classics in 1890. But from 1896 to 1926, his interests had been mainly administrative. He had acted as Tutor, Secretary to Council and Senate, Registrar, and finally as Senior Pro-Vice-Chancellor charged with many of the duties formerly left to the Vice-Chancellor himself. When, in 1926, Sir Walter Moberly came to be our Vice-Chancellor, the office of Senior Pro-Vice-Chancellor, in the special function in which it had been exercised by Fiddes, was suspended: and Fiddes took up again his scholarly interests as occupant of the Ward Chair of History. As might be suspected, Fiddes's volume is that of a man who has at his finger-tips all the official documentary material by virtue of which the University holds its status and conducts its daily life. He was a Scot with a practical cast of mind. Temperamentally, he was a realist. He was not passionately interested in the ultimate nature or in the ideal purpose of the University. He was much more eager to provide for it all the safeguards which would ensure that whatever it did was well done and was well worth the doing. It is greatly to be regretted that, with his unequalled knowledge of the workings of the University, he did not continue the history to a later time, for he lived in proximity to us until his death in 1942.

Another separate volume which is in some sense a history of Owens College is one edited by P. J. Hartog, *The Owens College, Manchester, (founded 1851) A Brief History of the College and Description of its various Departments* (Cornish, Manchester, 1901). Hartog had been a student of Owens from 1880 to 1882; he returned in 1889 as Bishop Berkeley Fellow in Chemical Physics. Later he was an assistant lecturer in Chemistry, and gradually went over to administrative duties, acting as Secretary to the University Extension Committee from 1895 until 1903, when he was appointed Academic Registrar of London University. In later life his work as an academic and public administrator brought its due reward: he became Sir Philip Hartog, K.B.E., C.I.E.

His volume was prepared in response to the organising committee of an Education Exhibition to be held in London in 1900. They wanted a factual record of the college as a working organisation, with details of the staffing of all departments, the facilities for study, the provision of scholarships and other such particulars. But as the jubilee of the college was near, the volume was introduced by a brief historical sketch—some twenty pages—of its origin and progress. The essential substance of the volume, however, is the formal information it provides about the constitution, the officers, the departments, the staff, the library, the fellows and the scholarship-holders, the publications of all teachers, and so forth. It is therefore a most useful reference book of information about the human and material resources of the college, the bulk of it given, properly, in lists and tables.

The Jubilee in 1901 did, however, provide printed materials much more helpful to an understanding of the organic characteristics of the Owens College of the day. They illustrate trends, opinions, and activities of the members of the collegiate community which bring the reader into closer touch with its academic habit and social sense than do statistical and graphical formulæ. The Jubilee directly sponsored the appearance of two volumes. One was a special number of *The Owens College Union Magazine*, issued as memoranda of the foregoing fifty years. It was entitled *The Owens College Jubilee* (Sherratt & Hughes, Manchester, 1901), and consisted of eighty large-sized pages, with some thirty illustrations, and about the same number of articles, all of which recalled what Owens had been at various stages of its fifty years' existence. The most interesting articles are not those written by the professors, but those contributed by former students. The Rev. J. Worthington's was " In 1851 and Later " ; Joseph Thompson's " Recollections of the Old College " ; George Harwood's " A Few Reminiscences and Conclusions " ; J. K. Wright's " Owens in the 60's " ; Henry Brierley's " Further Reminiscences of Owens College Forty Years Ago " ; Spenser Wilkinson's " Some College Friendships " ; J. T. Kay's " Notes on the History of the Union " ; R. Thorburn's " The Lacrosse Club " ; and two articles dealing with the entry of women students into the University, Miss E. Lang's " The Beginnings of the Women's Department ", and Miss Catherine Chisholm's " The Development of the Women's Department ".

The other Jubilee volume was a *Record of the Jubilee Celebrations at Owens College, Manchester* (Sherratt & Hughes, Manchester, 1902), and was issued by the Committee of *The Owens College Union Magazine* at the request of the Council of the College. (The formal and public commemoration of the Jubilee had been deferred from 1901 to 1902, since in 1902 there was to be an impressive ceremony for the opening of the Whitworth Hall by the Prince and Princess of Wales.) After a brief eighteen-page historical sketch by Miss Josephine Laidler, the volume describes in considerable detail all the ceremonies and gatherings arranged for the Jubilee and prints in full all the congratulatory addresses sent for the occasion by foreign and other universities.

Besides the books mentioned above, short, but authoritative, outline surveys of the history of the University have appeared as articles in volumes compiled for more general Manchester gatherings. A handbook, *Manchester in 1915* (Manchester University Press), was issued in connection with the meeting in Manchester of the British Association for the Advancement of Science ; it contained a thirteen-page article on the University by T. F. Tout. In 1929 the Society of Chemical Industry met in Manchester, and the Manchester Branch of it brought out a sizable volume, *The Soul of Manchester* (Manchester University Press, 1929), for the occasion. It contained a fifteen-page article on the University by F. E. Weiss.

But of all that has gone on happening in the University since 1914, there is no record comparable in purpose and size with the works of Thompson and Fiddes. The spirit of the University has been to think ahead rather than to look backward ; and thus it has largely let its own past take care of itself. Perhaps because ceremonies intrude on the working programme of the day, perhaps, too, because the University's historic nonconformist inheritance made it suspicious of any sort of repetitive ritual, even when such solemnities had a purely secular setting, the tradition of ceremonial celebration has grown but slowly into our habitual practice. Though from the beginning of Owens College, the opening and the close of the college session was marked by an official public meeting, such meetings were largely a part of routine administration. A review of the year's work would be presented ; prizes would be distributed ; the principal would make a speech, and one of the professors, preferably one new to the staff, would give an address on the place of his subject in the academic pattern of knowledge. But, down the years, only a few occasions were judged sufficiently important to merit formal commemorative celebration ; and by their very nature they were occasions which could not be of too frequent recurrence, the College Jubilee, the University Jubilee, the fiftieth or the twenty-fifth anniversary of this or the other department, or of some other significant academic body, such as the Training Department or the Department for Women. It was long before annually recurrent solemnities were instituted and established in due ceremonial form. To-day the most formal and impressive of our annual ceremonies is Founder's Day. But it is only very recently that it has established itself in our ritual, and even so, its establishment was the almost fortuitous conclusion of a series of experimental failures. As early as 1905 the students themselves had taken the initiative, and had petitioned Council to set aside a day for a Founder's Day ceremony. Council decided that it was not expedient to do so. In 1911, there was a proposal before Senate to hold annually a Memorial Service in the Cathedral. That seemed to some likely to stir the old Manchester sentiment against sectarian preferences : and a devout Anglican, Tout, moved that there be no official recognition of such a service. A later resolution approved of a Commemoration Service inside the secular precincts of the University. But when later in the year, more precise arrangements for the Commemoration Service to be held in the Whitworth Hall were discussed, Senate, with Tout again taking the lead, rescinded its previous resolution, and decided that no such service should be held. In the upshot, it was adventitiously that the matter arose again. It was a direct outcome of the European war. In 1916 the names of many of our staff and students had appeared in casualty lists, and it was felt that a ceremony to commemorate the fallen was in itself desirable and would also enhance the solemnity of a Founder's Day celebration. The solemn gathering took place in March 1917 and an oration was delivered by Sir Adolphus William Ward, Master of Peterhouse, former Principal of Owens College, and former Vice-Chancellor of Victoria University. The following year a similar service of commemoration for the University and for the fallen was held ; but when peace came, interest in a Founder's Day lapsed. A revival of it was discussed in 1920 ; it was linked with the suggestion that it should be associated with a religious service, which would not be held in the University, but in a church to which members of the University would be officially invited. Even in 1920 proposals of that sort again aroused something of the sectarian sentiments of the 1850's, and the plan was not pursued. A purely academic Founder's Day was, however, organised for a Saturday in February, 1922. Hardly anybody attended. It was, indeed, so depressing an event that the whole matter was submitted for consideration to a committee. As a result it was recommended that the linking of Founder's Day with an annual conferment of honorary degrees would provide the opportunity for a dignified academic ceremony at which some solemn recital, recalling our Founder and other benefactors, would be a fitting item. It was not, however, until 1932 that the formal ritual of the day was fully established, and that year, too, the simple dignified expression of the faith and the spirit of the University was worthily embodied in the Text of the Recital. Each year this is impressively read at the ceremony by the Vice-Chancellor :

" To-day we hold in grateful remembrance our founders and all our benefactors. In this place we live in a free and happy fellowship of common endeavour, and by this yearly commemoration we take thought how wide are the bounds of that fellowship. We unite ourselves in spirit with all our benefactors, both the dead and the living. We salute all those before us into whose labours we have entered, looking forward as they did to generations yet to come who, in their turn, will share this fellowship, and will give of their substance and of themselves to the advancement and dissemination of knowledge, and to the raising up of men and women nurtured and equipped for the service of the Commonwealth and of mankind.

" Such was John Owens, founder of Owens College and through it, of the University. His name and those of many others, who by their gifts and by their service, have fostered the growth and have advanced the welfare of our community, are inscribed upon the Roll of Founders and Benefactors of this, the Victoria University of Manchester. All these alike—both the renowned and the obscure, those who gave great gifts of their abundance and those who gave small gifts of their penury—we hold in honour to-day. By them, and by their like, our life has been enriched. Their bounty has borne fruit, and we commemorate with them those scholars and teachers who have brought fame to this place and have laid the foundations on which we build. Our high and firm endeavour is to be worthy of their trust and to make manifest in our time, even as they by word and deed have done before us, a sure and constant faith in the abiding virtue of spiritual things."

The definitive establishment of a canonical calendar, with rites and ceremonies for named days, is a strong link between the past and the future. To us of the present, it is a recurrent reassertion of the continuity and the identity of the corporate body of which we are a part. Amongst the red-letter days in such a calendar, jubilee days, whether of college or of university, none so far can have gathered to itself so much efficacy as this, our centenary, will gather. It will bring home to us how truly we are in spirit what in law Sir Alfred Hopkinson always insisted we were, members of a body whose corporate existence goes back unbrokenly to 1851, inheritors of the mission laid down for us by our Founder, to pursue the knowledge which is truth, and to vitalise it as a moral and scientific instrument in the service of man's essential and higher needs, and especially of such needs as present themselves in the society which peoples our regional environment. As our centenary will stir such thoughts within us, it may be hoped that it will bring home to us the need to set up forthwith a formal organisation for the gathering, the care, the arrangement of all relevant records of our past. It is imperative that the University should organise the preparation of a history worthy of itself. It will be a big undertaking and will involve some years of collaborative effort in the assembly of all the relevant material. It will mean the setting up, probably in the library, of a department of academic archives vastly larger in scope than are the printed formal records of decisions by Court or Council or Senate, on the one hand, or, on the other, the legal documents and deeds which confer on the University its status or entitle it to hold its various properties. For all such documents as these provide merely the skeleton, the bare anatomy ; to bring them to life and to understand them as autonomous energies one wants the physiology and the psychology of the organism. One wants not only reasons which lead to the adoption of resolutions, one wants even more the impulses and motives in the minds of the men and women who urged the resolutions. The preparatory mechanisms and the appropriate staff for gathering and arranging the vast variety of this larger range of necessary documentary evidence should be set up forthwith as a Centenary Memorial. Manchester University is known throughout the world for its studies in history : it cannot longer neglect the history of itself.

CHAPTER II

THE PREPARATION

FOR a hundred years before the foundation of Owens College, the intellectual atmosphere of Manchester was becoming more and more charged with spiritual forces which, as if spontaneously, had begun to realise themselves in learned societies and academic institutions. The mainsprings of these forces lie particularly in what was becoming the dominantly Mancunian frame of mind on religious, political and social questions. A fervent Nonconformity—presbyterian, methodist, congregational, baptist, unitarian, and Quaker—with its strong sense of freedom of thought and individual liberty, generated a political liberalism which insisted on the sacred rights of the individual, but recognised as categorical the obligation on individual man to render service to the general progress and well-being of society.

The Industrial Revolution brought home to Manchester men the material value of knowledge. Their social sense led them to see knowledge as a means to culture and civilisation. Their moral ideals turned them to projects for disseminating knowledge, not as exercises in benevolent altruism, but as indispensable instruments for the health of society and the progress of mankind. Similar movements were, of course, stirring in other parts of the kingdom : but it was in the new industrial cities of the North that they acquired their special character and vigour. Hence there arose in Manchester between 1780 and 1851, a number of institutions, organisations, societies, and academies all of which were, in the widest sense, educational ventures. Amongst them were *The Literary and Philosophical Society* (1781); *The College of Arts and Science* (1783); *The Manchester Academy* (1786); *The New College* (1793) (in which Dalton taught until it went to York about 1800); *The Natural History Society* (1821); *The Royal Manchester Institution* (1824); *The Mechanics' Institution* (1824); *The Royal Medical College* (1824); and *The Manchester Statistical*

Society (1833). The activities of these many institutions were widely varied. Some were learned societies in the sense current to-day ; others were educational organisations with specific purposes, *The Mechanics' Institution*, for instance, and, in its own way, *The Royal Manchester Institution*. Others had a more comprehensive educational programme, even a collegiate teaching scheme of higher education, like *The College of Arts and Science, The New College*, and, in its own field, *The Royal Medical School*. Yet all these, in their own kind, were preparing the ground for Owens College and experimenting in functions which, with modified articulation, were to be incorporated later in the intellectual structure of Owens College. Moreover, most of them were directly the outcome of the particular social and political circumstance which in due course prompted the setting up of Owens College. Many of them were academic organisations primarily for the education of nonconformist ministers, since the older universities were effectively closed to them by the religious Tests. But these nonconformist academies did not restrict their admissions to intending ministers ; they admitted all who wished to be pupils. Amongst their students, naturally, were many sons of nonconformists who were not being brought up to enter the ministry, but for business or for a secular profession.

The progress to Owens College can be followed in a series of projects put forward publicly through, or in connection with, some of the organisations mentioned above. Historically, as is commonly known, the first formal proposal for the institution of a University of Manchester was made in 1640. A public meeting commissioned Henry Fairfax to write to his elder brother, Lord Fairfax, imploring his aid in the presentation of a petition to the Long Parliament. The Petition states how much the North suffers through having no Northern University—" many ripe and hopeful wits being utterly lost for want of education, some being unable, others unwilling, to commit their children of tender and unsettled age so far from their own eyes, to the sole care and tuition of strangers ". It humbly submits the following reasons for the Petition ; the great distance from the North to either Oxford or Cambridge ; the great charges of these universities ; the expectation that gentlemen of the northern regions would be moved to liberal benefactions in support of a provincial university. It then states its claim for Manchester as the place for the new university—" we apprehend Manchester to be the fittest place for such a foundation, it being almost the centre of these northern parts, a town of great antiquity, formerly both a city and a sanctuary, and now of great fame and ability, by the happy traffic of its inhabitants, for its situation, provision of food, fuel and buildings as happy as any town in the northern parts of the Kingdom. To all this we add the convenience of the college there already built, both large and ancient and now, as we understand, intended to this purpose by the piety and munificence of the Right Honourable James, Lord Strange, a noble encourager of this great work." The Petition was unsuccessful. The Civil War began and at the end of it, Cromwell gave the North a university at Durham, and, naturally, this was abolished at the Restoration. Had the Petition succeeded, Manchester University would have been on the spot which a little later became Chetham's Library and Hospital. The really significant features of this petition are its insistence on the notion of a regional university, serving regional needs and drawing on local sympathy, and its claim that the costs must be low so that it is available to those who are not wealthy. The motives which inspired John Owens and his friends were clearly deeply ingrained in the *genius loci*.

The approach to Owens College has gone much further when we come to the next public proposal for a Manchester college. In 1783, Arthur Thomas Barnes, D.D., Presbyterian Minister at Cross Street Chapel, read a paper to the Literary and Philosophical Society on " A Plan for the Improvement and Extension of Liberal Education in Manchester ". It advocated a " plan of liberal education for young men designed for civil and active life, whether in trade or in any of the professions ". He recommended a syllabus liberal in the traditional sense but including " law and commerce ". Whilst " connecting together liberal science and commercial industry " and affording a training for the learned professions as well as for commerce, the object was to give the adolescent student " that degree of knowledge and taste, which may make him more than the mere man of business in future life ". It would carefully avoid " giving to the students views, habits and tastes which may be unsuitable for a man of business ". There is, too, a fundamental item : as " science and arts are of no political or religious party ", there was to be no political or religious exclusiveness. Dr. Barnes's project came into existence as the College of Arts and Sciences in 1783. When a somewhat similar organisation, the Manchester Academy, was instituted in 1786, Dr. Barnes gave the inaugural address, and still further revealed the spirit which inspired these projects. " Educated in the principles of liberty, civil and religious, and deeming those principles essential to every higher interest of man ", its founders had brought into being a " Seminary of Education which shall breathe the same spirit, which shall thus serve, in the most effectual manner, the cause of truth and goodness ".   The institution is formed " upon the most liberal and generous basis, guarded by no jealous subscription ", and open to all " who wish to enjoy the advantages of science unfettered and free ".   " You regard it as your duty, you demand it as your birthright, you glory in it as your privilege, to judge for yourselves on every subject of science, and, above all, of religion, and act according to your own convictions."   " You plead for the equal universal dominion of reason, of conscience, and of truth, and to these great interests alone you consecrate this seminary."   He proceeded to comment on the programme of studies, laid out as " affording a full and systematic course of education for divines, and preparatory instruction for other learned professions, as well as for civil and commercial life."   Of particular interest, in the light of the future, are his speculations on higher education for men of business.   " I imagine to myself a system of education for a commercial man which shall contain all the parts of science proper for him to know, as much as possible in a practical form, and which amidst all the other objects of study shall keep this point continually in view.   In this system the several noble Arts on which Commerce depends are illustrated by their respective Sciences, whilst Science again is rendered clear and entertaining by its application to the Arts.   Shall young men of every other class have studies and discipline peculiar to themselves, and shall the man of Business, the Merchant, who will be called to sustain so very interesting and honourable a character among his fellow-citizens, be improved by no studies, be formed by no discipline, be trained by no habits which more immediately belong to his future province ?   The present learned and worthy Bishop of Llandaff has lately proposed to introduce lectures upon Agriculture and Commerce into the Universities [i.e. into Oxford and Cambridge, for when ' the present learned and worthy bishop ' spoke, England and Wales had only two universities, Oxford and Cambridge].   It would be some advance towards that ideal scheme, the faint and imperfect outline of which imagination has drawn before me."

It has seemed fitting to set forth these schemes of Dr. Barnes at some length because they indicate how the Manchester situation is beginning to articulate itself and thus to clarify the nature of the ideals which first stimulated the Manchester method of meeting that situation.   The ideas

THE SENATE 1862–1863

Reading from left to right: H. E. ROSCOE, A. SANDEMAN, R. C. CHRISTIE, R. B. CLIFTON,
J. G. GREENWOOD, A. J. SCOTT, T. THEODORES, W. C. WILLIAMSON.

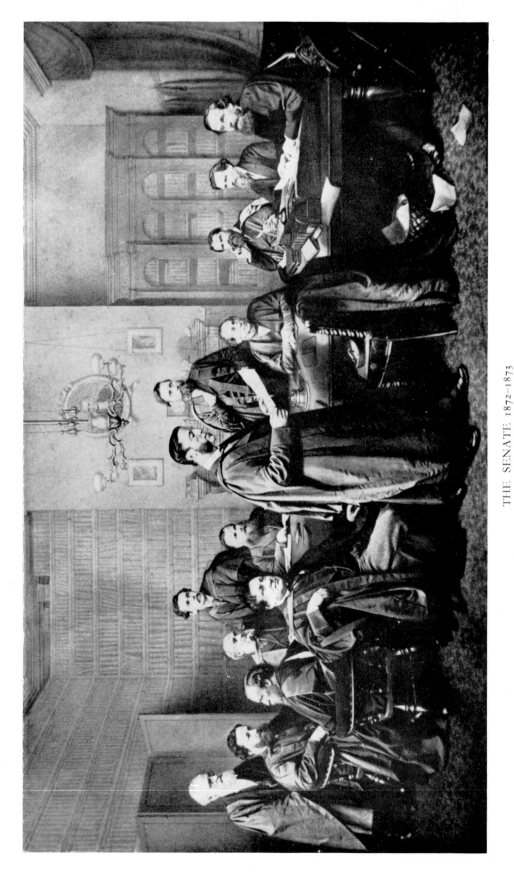

THE SENATE 1872–1873

Reading from left to right : W. C. WILLIAMSON, W. S. JEVONS, T. H. CORE, BALFOUR STEWART, A. S. WILKINS, H. E. ROSCOE, T. BARKER, A. W. WARD, O. REYNOLDS, T. THEODORES, J. BRYCE, J. H. NICHOLSON (*Registrar*), J. G. GREENWOOD.

and the intentions are more significant than the particular institutions in which they were embodied in Dr. Barnes's time.

Although the ferment of progressive educational and social ideals continued to agitate the minds of Manchester's leading citizens during the generation following that of Barnes, and produced the series of learned and cultural societies already named, it was not until 1829 that the next organised attempt was made to set up a university in Manchester. The Royal Institution of Manchester had been established in 1824, mainly to serve as an Art Gallery and Museum in the days when exhibitions of works of art were purposively organised as instruments of progressive culture. W. R. Whatton was a Governor of the Royal Institution, and in 1829, in two documents, an Address and a second Letter, he proposed to his fellow-governors the extension of the functions of the Royal Institution to form a University of Manchester. But despite the general soundness of his plea, there is lacking in it that fervour of passionate conviction to which Manchester men were more likely to respond : the most powerful appeal to a northerner is one in which the imagination discloses to the intellect a possibility which arouses a passion in him to achieve what he will regard as a moral ideal. Whatton reflects " that within a circle whose radius is only twenty miles, there are contained little less than two millions of souls, a mass equal to the population of a similar space round the metropolis of the Empire ". " The wants of the great mass of these people speak plainly in favour of the establishment of some good and efficient system of education." So far, the sentiment was a commonplace of Manchester thought. But his elaboration of it strikes no congenial spark. " Such a system, conducted on liberal principles, I contend, would ameliorate men's feelings and desires ; would improve the social order of the multitude ; would strengthen the hands of a wise and good government, and enhance the general happiness by making man content with himself, by arming his soul against the snares of prosperity, and by enabling him to meet, with resignation and fortitude, the trials and pressures of adversity." A missionary needs a more fiery gospel than this to excite his congregation's zeal. In any event, the Royal Institution, concerned primarily with the Fine Arts, was hardly the most suitable starting-point and nucleus for the kind of university which Manchester would demand. There is a good deal of reason in the details of Whatton's plans. His syllabus, in its tripartite grouping of Literature, Science, and the Arts, is liberal and comprehensive. He is not unmindful of the necessity of linking learning with local industrial needs. He recognises and accepts the Manchester view of religious tests, and, evading the real problem behind this, merely omits theology as a subject from his syllabus ; " the religious education of the students must be left to the domestic care of their natural guardians ". Though he includes the classical languages in his plan, he havers about their real function—" if a man have leisure to accomplish himself in ancient literature, nobody denies the refinement and pleasure of the acquisition ; all the people doubt is whether its advantages compensate to a man who must economise time in his education, for the heavy sacrifice of so many years as are commonly bestowed on learning Greek and Latin ".

On the whole, therefore, Whatton marks no major progress towards the idea of Manchester University, though he is, so to speak, a museum piece exemplifying the characteristics of the Manchester problem.

The real step forward came through the activities of another group of representative Manchester citizens, those who originated in 1833 the Manchester Statistical Society, which still flourishes, and moreover was first of its kind in England. The main object of the founders of the Statistical Society was to apply statistical methods to the study and to the solution of the social problems of their day : they promoted a series of social surveys, and education was one of the chief of their interests. Bankers, merchants, and manufacturers formed the main body of the society and their common bond was a keen civic consciousness and a sense of public duty. At the invitation of the Statistical Society in 1836, H. L. Jones, a former Fellow of Magdalene College, Cambridge, read to it a paper on a proposal to institute a University in Manchester. The paper was published with the title *Plan of a University for the Town of Manchester*, by Harry Longworth Jones, M.A. (Manchester, Robert Robinson, 1836). The costs of publication were paid by one of the brothers Heywood, members of a Manchester banker family. He was the James Heywood who was later named by John Owens in his will as a trustee for the Owens trust fund : later still, when he had become Member of Parliament for North Lancashire, he was a leading member of the group which during the 'fifties was mainly concerned with promoting parliamentary measures which would make Oxford and Cambridge as free from religious tests as Owens had made Manchester. H. L. Jones was not a Manchester man, and his Manchester scheme was apparently a speculative result of his feeling of dissatisfaction with the older universities, and their increasing separation from the life of their generation. He wanted to see universities arise in the great centres of population, as was beginning to happen on the Continent. In that way more people could more easily avail themselves of their benefits ; and in turn the universities could have direct awareness of the problems of their immediate province. Hence he had naturally thought of Manchester. " In all directions the circle of Manchester is full of life and intelligence ; manufactures of every kind occupy the inhabitants of the towns ; the movement of money is immense ; commercial activity is carried to an extraordinary pitch ; mechanical ingenuity receives there daily new developments ; the minds of men are in a state of electric communication of ideas ; their political sentiments indicate the restless vigour of a rising and strong people ; their religious opinions are full of fervour and piety."

The plans he expounded had powerful repercussions. He was talking to men who were business men and statisticians, and he presented to them a clear and comprehensive practical scheme. He did not in fact propound any notions which had hitherto not been part of the existing currents of Manchester educational thought. But advancing his proposals as rational deductions, he seemed to give general philosophic validity to what had been urgently and intuitively felt as immediate and local needs. He had chiefly in mind the education of " that part of the population which is rising into manhood, and is destined for the higher branches of commercial occupation or for the learned professions ". The University must embrace knowledge in all its branches ; moreover, its framework should allow for the expansion of knowledge proportionate to the demands of the times. The education given should be " as wide and universal as circumstances will admit ; not that, in the dispensing of it, it should become vague and desultory—for that is not education ". The teaching must be kept as " free as possible from degenerating into a system of authority ", for the student " should be a searcher after information, rather than a passive recipient of it ". The University should admit persons of all religious persuasions, and as far as possible the University should provide religious instruction and guidance for each student in his own system of belief. " More truth is developed from the collision of many than from the incumbent pressure of a single theological system." " Teachers of religion ought to be selected from the most efficient and talented ministers of the principal denominations in the neighbourhood, and accommodation found for the delivery of their lectures under the sanction of the University." That is exactly the way, in which, sixty-seven years later, Manchester University established a Faculty of Theology : its spirit could not be more finely summarised than in Jones's sentence, " more truth is developed from the collision of many than from the incumbent pressure of a single theological system ". It is the spirit of Milton's *Areopagitica*, and of all gospels of toleration and freedom.

Moreover, whilst the traditional subjects of university education obviously must be provided, " some special application of certain kinds of knowledge should be made to the particular circumstances of the case. Thus the district of Manchester is a commercial and manufacturing one : and its inhabitants, of whatever rank, are much occupied in the different callings connected with the prevailing characteristics of the county. Hence in such a University, provision should be made for affording information on subjects connected with commerce, with arts and manufacture, and the student's attention should not be so entirely occupied with the severer parts of academic education as not to be devoted to the cultivation, in due time and place, of knowledge that may be useful to him in the probable occupation of his future life. Thus, for example, great encouragement should be given in the University of Manchester to the study of mathematical science, of political and social history, and of the practical application of mathematics and calculation to the affairs of banking and commercial operations." Further the University should have two different kinds of courses, one for the regular body of students who will receive their teaching in the day time, and the other for those " who may be desirous of devoting the time not occupied by business to the improvement and cultivation of their minds, and for this second group evening lectures will be necessary ". The regular students were to follow a continuous three-year course, periodically tested by examinations, and leading to a final examination.

Jones's real service, as we have said, was not in bringing novel ideas ; but in translating into a practicable structure a group of purposes of which Manchester had been increasingly and more fervently conscious, the need for a modern university, possessing full intellectual freedom, actively associated with the life and work of the area ; a non-residential university available for the collegiate education of a new social group or series of groups. His paper led to the calling of a General Meeting of Citizens, and steps were taken to draft proposals for action.

Jones had given his audience a concrete idea of the academic structure of a college. His scheme of subjects of study included zoology, though he saw it as something which at first need not be provided. When it was, it would include anatomy and physiology. It naturally occurred to the committee that Manchester already had a successful Medical School, giving systematic teaching in medicine, anatomy, physiology, pathology and the related sciences : indeed this school, founded and owned and directed by Thomas Turner, F.R.C.S., was officially permitted in 1824 to call itself the Manchester Royal School of Medicine. Here then, was a collegiate institution, and it might well provide a model for the more general college, or it might even collaborate with it. Indeed, even as early as 1836, an alliance or amalgamation between the proposed new college and the Royal School of Medicine was being discussed under favourable auspices, and the negotiations to that end might well have succeeded. But the Royal School's supremacy was being challenged by other medical teaching bodies, and the committee for the proposed university college suspended further action. It is also not unlikely that interest in the city itself lapsed because its most active group of citizens, those members of the Statistical Society who had instigated Jones's paper, were themselves much more occupied in the middle 'thirties with a different, and, socially, a wider problem of education. They were preparing and issuing reports on various features of elementary education, especially in Manchester, and Salford, and other Lancashire towns. They exposed the extreme inadequacy of the means of primary education ; and the low quality of the teachers and of their teaching. They urged the establishment of training colleges, and were aiming ultimately to arouse the public conscience to compel the State to take wider responsibilities for the people's education. But a city which had within it families like the Heywoods, the Langtons, the Gregs, and the Hopkinsons was only awaiting the opportunity which was to be provided by John Owens' bequest. The purpose and the nature of the college they would wish, and its rôle in the progress of its provincial society, was well established in the general mind.

CHAPTER III

THE FOUNDATION

JOHN OWENS, born in Manchester in 1790, was the son of Owen Owens who had left his native Flintshire in adolescence to seek his fortune in the industry of Manchester. Success came early, the reward of his frugality and enterprise. He could afford to send his son John to a private day-school on Ardwick Green ; and, presumably when the lad was about fourteen, he went into his father's firm, " Owen Owens, 9 Carpenter's Lane, hat-linings, currier and furrier ". The son was partner before 1819 for, in that year, the title of the firm had been changed to " Owen Owens and Son, manufacturers ". The undertaking prospered ; and John Owens widened his own commercial interests with other ventures ; for a time, for example, he was partner in the cotton-spinning firm of Samuel Faulkner, whose son George had from schooldays become his closest and perhaps his only intimate friend. John Owens remained a bachelor to the end of his life ; there are rumours of a decorous flirtation which was ended by the lady's death. He lived in his father's home at 9 Nelson Street, Chorlton-upon-Medlock. Fiddes, in his book on the University, summarises the meagre information which can be drawn from the available accounts of John Owens. But the yield is small. There is an account, not mentioned by Fiddes, in Volume 10 of *The Owens College Magazine* (1877–78). Though it adds nothing to the available stock of facts, there are one or two paragraphs in it pertinent to the trend of our argument, namely that it was the spirit of Manchester which through the material instrumentality of John Owens was in effect founding its own college. The author of the *Magazine* article tries to rescue Owens' name from oblivion.

" To most of us he is now, only twenty-seven years after the opening of the College, nothing more than a name. At the first glance it seems extraordinary that so little should be known of him in Manchester, where he was born and lived all his life, and where he was at the head of a firm doing a large amount of business. Yet the fact may be explained without difficulty. There are not many incidents in the life of a man entirely given up to business in a great city like Manchester which attract notice or are of interest to more than his immediate circle of friends. And Mr. Owens' circle was very limited. His business was a foreign one, and probably did not necessitate much intercourse between its principal and leading business men in Manchester. To this must be added that he was a man of very retiring habits : he kept no company whatever ; his only friend seems to have been George Faulkner ; and his housekeeper told Mr. Nicholson when, early in the history of the College, he tried to collect all the information he could about Mr. Owens, that he used to spend his evenings quietly at home, amusing himself with his books. She always speaks of him as a man of very reserved habits, differing very much from his father, who was a genial, hearty man. [The University Library has a curious piece of testimony to this temperamental difference between John Owens and Owen Owens, his father. It owns a copy of Scholes's *Manchester and Salford Directory* (1797), which, on the authority of Thomas Mattinson, John Owens' clerk, belonged to Owen Owens. The striking thing about the volume is this. There are inserted crosses against all names associated with businesses like that of Owen Owens ; but the only other markings in the volume are scorings under the names of every public house in the Directory. Both on historical and psychological grounds, it is improbable that these underlinings were made in the spirit of a Welshman's teetotal fanaticism. One hopes, of course, that they were not added by someone after the volume came to our library.] Probably his moodiness was to a large extent due to bad health, as he was often ailing. There was, therefore, nothing to call attention to him till after his death. Even then, it was nearly five years before the College was opened, and probably it was not for several years more that any large section of the Manchester public began to recognise the importance of the institution which was growing up in their midst."

Even in the literal sense, the proposal and the planning of the foundation was a co-operative suggestion. Although George Faulkner, a Conservative Anglican, is with reasonable probability held to have prompted Owens, when he was making his will, to endow a college, the notion itself could have been no strange one to a Manchester mind. Moreover, John Owens himself made the designing of the foundation

c

and the control of it a co-operative effort of men whom he regarded as representative of the city and of its ideals.

He made his will in May, 1845. And for a man of his political persuasion, an advanced Liberal, 1845 was an exciting year. The Manchester agitation for the Repeal of the Corn Laws was working towards its triumphant close. In 1845, an Anti-Corn-Law Bazaar was held in the Free Trade Hall to raise money for the £100,000 Repeal fund. In the same year, Manchester Town Council decided to buy the manorial rights of the town from Sir Oswald Mosley. In 1845, also, Her Majesty's Government opened the first Bonding Warehouse in Manchester for the Manchester trade. During the same year, Peel Park, Salford, Queen's Park, Harpurhey, and Philips Park were bought by the private funds of a committee set up to establish public parks in Manchester. In March, 1845, Sir Thomas Potter died; he had borne the main brunt of the fight for incorporation and had been the first mayor of Manchester; besides his large municipal activities, Potter had established and maintained a day-school for boys and girls at Irlam o' th' Heights. Clearly, therefore, the testamentary benevolence of a man like Owens might have been directed in such a year as 1845 to any of the purposes prompted by the happening of these and such-like events at the moment when he was thinking of his will, for so many of them were efforts towards the particular forms of social amelioration which attracted the liberal mind. But John Owens' will makes it clear that it was through education that, in his belief, the main instrument of social progress was to be secured, and that education must therefore be the social instrument he should endow. Yet even in the field of education he might have chosen other schemes than that of a college. The foundation-stone of the Manchester Commercial Schools in Stretford Road was laid in 1845. The first of a series of concerts for the working classes, conducted by the committee of the Lancashire and Cheshire Philharmonic Institution, was held in the Free Trade Hall in April, 1845. But John Owens, in the interests of commercial and social well-being, wanted more than a school of commerce, and something more substantial than philanthropic experiments in æsthetic elevation for the masses. Moreover, the trend, during the 'forties, of the movement which sought to establish a national system of elementary education would have been sufficient to make him hesitant to give his means to the support of popular elementary education. In 1839 four Cabinet Ministers had been constituted a committee to superintend the grant by the Government (£20,000 a year divided between the two societies who regarded themselves as the organisers of public elementary education, the Anglican " National Society " and the nominally unsectarian, but predominantly nonconformist, " British and Foreign School Society "). The secretary of this committee, the precursor of the Ministry of Education, was Dr. Kay, the Manchester physician, member of the Manchester Literary and Philosophical Society, and of the Manchester Statistical Society, the man who became Sir James Kay-Shuttleworth, and of whom Sir Michael Sadler said—" to him more than to anyone else we owe it that England is supplied with schools for the children of her people, and that this costly work has been accomplished without a break between Church and State ". But in his first decade of office, the 'forties, sectarianism seemed likely to frustrate all his efforts. As Brougham wittily said : " The Church was anxious to educate the people, but the Church was still more anxious to get the better of the sects ; the sects were anxious to have popular education, but the sects were still more anxious than this to overturn the Church." John Owens may well have shared Brougham's suspicions. Without recanting his nonconformist creed, he had left his Mosley Street Chapel because his individual right to the privacy of his own pew had been invaded. After that, he regularly worshipped in an Anglican Church, and was buried in the graveyard of St. John's in Deansgate, though there is neither likelihood nor evidence of his having been confirmed into the Anglican communion.

Taking all these circumstances of 1845 into account it does not seem difficult to imagine how, in drafting his will, John Owens chose to endow the foundation of a college for higher academic education which, as its main motive, should break down all forms of preferential sectarianism.

In his last will, signed in 1845, he appointed George Faulkner and Samuel Alcock as executors, and named a group of his acquaintances as trustees for what was to be the main residuary legacy, a trust for " educational purposes hereinafter appointed ". The named trustees were to be usually resident within fifty miles of Manchester, and were to be disqualified if they went elsewhere to live. Among the persons nominated some were chosen for their public office, the Mayor, the Dean, the Members of Parliament for Manchester ; the rest were his friends or acquaintances, George Faulkner, Samuel Alcock, William Neild, James Heywood, Alexander Kay, Samuel Fletcher, Richard Cobden, John Benjamin Smith, John Frederick Foster and Mark Philips. Most of them were, like the testator, men engaged in Manchester industry or commerce, and all but two or three were men associated with the Manchester fashion of liberal thought. Only three of them had been to an English university, the Dean, James Heywood, and Frederick Foster. It is, however, worth noting that the one of them who was most intimate with Owens, George Faulkner, was a conservative and an Anglican. Altogether, the trustees named did fairly represent the more characteristic forms of the social thinking which prevailed amongst the Manchester men of the time. On these trustees Owens laid the task of working out all details for the foundation, the organisation, the appropriate staffing and the most suitable pattern of curricula for the institution which would realise the general principles enunciated in his will. They were trustees appointed to carry into effect " my earnest desire and general object to found within the said parliamentary borough of Manchester, or within two miles from any part of the limits thereof, an institution for providing or aiding the means of instructing and improving young persons of the male sex (and being of an age not less than fourteen years) in such branches of learning and science as are now and may be hereafter usually taught in the English Universities, but subject nevertheless to the two fundamental and immutable rules and conditions hereinafter prescribed, namely : First, that the students, professors, teachers, and other officers and persons connected with the said institution, shall not be required to make any declaration as to, or submit to any test whatsoever of, their religious opinions, and that nothing shall be introduced in the matter or mode of education or instruction in reference to any religious or theological subject which shall be reasonably offensive to the conscience of any student, or of his relations, guardians, or friends, under whose immediate care he shall be. Secondly, that if, and as often as, the number of applicants for admission to such institution as students shall be more than adequate to the means of the institution, a preference shall in all cases be given to the children of parents residing, or who, if dead, or the survivor of whom, resided when living within the limits now comprised in the parliamentary borough of Manchester aforesaid, or within two miles from any part of such limits ; and secondly, to the children of parents residing, or who, or the survivor of whom when living, resided within the limits comprised in the parliamentary district or division of South Lancashire ; but subject as aforesaid, the said institution shall be open to all applicants for admission, without respect to place of birth, and without distinction of rank or condition in society."

A. J. SCOTT, PRINCIPAL 1851–1857

In a later part of the will, he indicates how the " conscience " clause should be made effective. If a complaint is made by or on behalf of any student, that offence is being given to his conscience, the complaint shall be sustained if one-third of the Trustees approve it, a condition illustrating that mingling of idealist and realist in John Owens, whose ideals made him see that " conscience " pleas are always in a minority, but whose business sense caused him to see that a limit must be set to the allowance made for them. One further direction is important : it indicates that he meant the money to be expended in securing the right men to carry on the academic work of the college rather than on the setting up of expensive buildings.

Such was the scheme : it expressed, as Sir Alfred Hopkinson said at the College Jubilee in 1901, " a plain Manchester merchant's ideal of what he would like a college in a great town to be ". The main features of that ideal are clear. The college is to be a non-residential institution primarily for teaching. Its teaching is to include such branches of knowledge as are, or may be, recognised university subjects ; it is teaching meant specifically for the people of its own region and mainly, therefore, for a new social group. For many, if not most, of these it would be the only means of systematic higher education : the older universities were too far away and otherwise too expensive ; moreover, Oxford and Cambridge were only open to them, even if they had means to go there, if their conscience allowed them to subscribe to the Anglican creed. Finally, Owens was to be a college for the education of males.

The Trustees had to translate these ideals into a working organisation. They took the task very seriously and very intelligently. On 30th January, 1849, the body of Trustees appointed a sub-committee to " take into consideration the general character and plan of the institution to be founded in pursuance of the directions of the Testator ; and the Branches of learning and Science to be taught therein ". Only one of the five members of the sub-committee had had any university education, and, though they eagerly sought and took advice from academic people, the plan they produced was essentially their own plan, a project devised for Manchester by the lay mind of typical Manchester men of commerce and of affairs. They did their work magnificently. At the outset, they saw that, above all, it was to Scotland that they should look for suggestions, for while the Scottish Universities " are intended and well fitted to embrace the education of youth of the highest ranks of society, their institutions have in no respect been framed or modified with reference to the means, or pursuits, or habits of the aristocracy : their system is that of a general plan of education by which persons of all ranks may be equally benefited. They have always embraced students of every variety and description, persons engaged in the actual occupations of business, who expect to derive aid in their pursuit from the new applications of science to the arts, or young men, not intended for any learned profession, or even going through any regular course of university education, but sent for one or more years to college, in order to carry their education further than that of the schools before they are engaged in the pursuits of trade or of commerce. Possessing these features, the Scotch Universities seem well adapted to afford suggestions for the plan of our intended institution."

In that frame of mind, the sub-committee first asked themselves what subjects were the backbone of a traditional university education. They found that they were the Classical Languages and Literatures, Mathematics, and Natural Philosophy (which is still the Scottish name for Physics). They examined the suitability of each of these departments of knowledge to become subjects in Owens College. They had no doubts about including in the first place the classical languages, and, moreover, for virtues in them expressed by their academic adviser, Whewell, of Trinity, as the " means of giving distinctness to men's ideas of the analogy of language, which distinctness is one main element of intellectual cultivation ". Clearly, these Manchester trustees were not iconoclasts : perhaps their real mind appears in this paragraph : " In a locality where men's minds and exertions are mainly devoted to commercial pursuits, it seems particularly desirable to select as an instrument of mental training a subject, which, being general in its nature, and remote from the particular and daily occupations of the individual, may counteract their tendency to limit the application and, eventually, the power of applying the mental faculties."

Mathematics must of course come in, both " as an instrument of mental discipline and improvement ", and also as capable of " application to the wants of a manufacturing district ".

Natural Philosophy or Physical Science claimed a place because, as largely mathematical in its nature, it had similar value " as a general mental discipline ", and also because in its many component parts, as for instance, in Chemistry it had " practical importance in reference to particular pursuits ".

On Mental and Moral Philosophy as an item in the normal curriculum, the academic advice they received was too contradictory to be directly helpful. Scotland did include this as an undergraduate subject, but others regarded the subject as not suitable to be " made the groundwork of education ". The advice which seems to have determined the inclusion of the subject came from Dr. Vaughan, of the Lancashire Independent College : " one of the great wants of modern Europe is that the masculine good sense of Englishmen should be brought to bear on those subtle speculations and weighty moral questions which are now elaborated elsewhere . . . to ends so much more mischievous than useful. Lancashire, if not so materialised as reported in some quarters, would certainly not be the worse for being brought a little more under the influence of a spiritualized philosophy, as preliminary to something still higher."

The last major subject which the committee thought essential to a " regular course of instruction for the general cultivation and discipline of the mind, and to prepare the student for advantageously applying to and effectively restoring any particular department of knowledge " was English Language and Literature, though in their recommendation for its inclusion, the stress is laid entirely on the discipline of general grammar in the achievement of " the accuracy of language which is essential to accuracy of reasoning ". As Professor of English Literature in Manchester University since 1921, I applaud the committee's wisdom, though now in 1950, I should put the case differently. Literature is what emerges from a special use of language : and in the end what matters is the extent to which language so used can enlarge mankind's awareness of reality.

In addition to these five primary subjects, the committee is prepared to add, as useful secondaries, Natural History and some of the modern languages. Although in their choice of the traditional subjects as the groundwork of a general education such as John Owens had intended, they had considered in each case the suitability and possible applicability of such subjects to the mind, the interest, and the pursuits of their regional population, they were unwilling to do as King's College was prepared to do in London for some of its students, namely, to confine a " general " course to nothing but what fitted in with the direct commercial or professional requirements of " applied scientists " : " we should greatly depreciate the sacrificing of the general to a particular course of instruction ".

The needs of the district, however, would be by no means forgotten. Students " not intending to go through the regular course ", could attend classes in such subjects as they deemed useful for their training as " engineers, machinists and other pursuits in practical science ". More-over, " as a large proportion of the students will probably consist of sons of merchants " something will be done to provide " instruction in the principles and elements of such departments of knowledge as are most generally subservient to the purposes of commercial life ". Still further, " considering the age at which young men in this district are usually engaged in business, there may, probably will be, a large body of students being desirous of improving themselves in the several subjects of the regular course, but unable to devote to their studies the period which may be required for a course extending to the higher departments of those subjects ". It was therefore recommended that in appropriate subjects, there should be two distinct courses, a lower and a higher grade, to meet local needs such as were occasioned by this feature of Lancashire's com-mercial and social habit. Even more emphatically directed to purposes of this kind was the recommendation that, although chemistry was part of a subject, Natural Philosophy, which was already incorporated in the basic scheme and had its professor, it would nevertheless be " expedient to appoint a Professor of Chemistry, to give not only elementary instruc-tion, but also a more extended course in chemical science generally, and as applied to the arts, with a view to afford greater facilities than at present exist in this neighbourhood, for obtaining instruction in a branch of science of so much local importance as well as general interest ". Man-chester was thus brought one stage nearer to the idea of a university in which technology is a really academic subject.

This phase of John Owens' intention, his insistence on identifying the college with its environment, provides other examples of the way in which the inherent idea propels novel activities which incorporate themselves, in modes varying with progressive circumstances, into the essential tradition of the college. For it not only directed attention to the scientific principles underlying the practical arts of the vicinity, it realised that social circumstance and habit would make it necessary to offer not only daytime, but evening courses of instruction. In the earliest years of the college there were more evening than day students. Figures, however, are somewhat misleading. It is easy nowadays to count numbers of students because in these days "student" is generally taken, in official academic phrasing, to mean a person registered as an undergraduate working for a degree. In the early years of the college, few students followed a com-

J. G. GREENWOOD, Principal 1857–1889

prehensively organised system of studies, in fact, few besides those day students who were working for a London University external degree. In the first decade of Owens, professors of the college had helped in the lecturing at the Working Men's College held at the Manchester Mechanics' Institute, and when in 1861 that college closed down, Owens College extended its evening classes to comprise others planned to suit the curriculum of a Working Men's College. Prior to that, its main evening activity had been the conduct of a series of courses for local schoolmasters whose own teaching occupied their daytime hours. Up to 1873 evening classes were accepted as part of the day's work by almost all the professors : in the session 1872–73 there were, as day-students, 334 studying Arts, Law, and Science, 112 medical students, and 557 evening students. It looks as if, until 1873, the evening work of the professors was gratuitous : but in 1873 steps were taken to endow evening classes. The situation changed when the Victoria University came into being in 1880 : it meant a more rigid distinction between the students attending day classes according to the regulations controlling its own or London's degree courses, and the more definitely occasional evening student who followed one or two courses according to his particular preference, none of which formally would lead to a degree. The result was a gradual decline in numbers at evening classes ; and although in the first Government Grant to Owens College (1889) the Treasury almost demanded that some of it should be used to subsidise evening classes, the Senate saw the opportunity to consolidate the traditional notion of a university as a place in which full-time study, prolonged over a fixed number of years, is the avenue to an academic degree. Hence Senate connived at and even assisted in the limitation of evening courses, though, recognising an academic extra-mural obligation, they increased the number of separate popular evening lectures. After Manchester became an independent university in 1903, there was a certain amount of public agitation for the establishment of evening courses which would lead to the degrees of B.A. and B.Sc. The College of Technology, by 1905 a part of the Faculty of Technology within the University, appealed for this principle in the preliminary negotiations of 1904 ; in 1905 the Association of Manchester Schoolmasters did the same ; in 1907 Sheffield University made overtures to its sister institution in Manchester to recognise evening courses for degrees ; our own Convocation in 1908 pleaded for degrees available to evening students who spread their studies over five years. In the next

year, some sort of compromise was proposed : the first (Intermediate)
Arts year might be followed by attendance at evening classes. Even as
late as 1921 the National Union of Teachers petitioned for the B.A. and
B.Sc. to be open to evening students. But, throughout, the Senate was
adamant. It had, however, in 1903 dealt with the problem in a novel
and characteristic way. Built round its Department of Economics, a
Faculty of Commerce had been set up and the University recognised that,
both in commerce and administration, many of the students would be
engaged in commercial and administrative pursuits during the daytime.
Moreover, when the chair of Economics had been endowed in 1866, the
endowment had been conditional on there being at least one evening
course. In 1903, a scheme was adopted in which there were to be alternative classes, the day ones being duplicated in the evening. The B.Com.,
which is now called B.A.(Com.) or B.A.(Admin.), is still the only degree
which the University awards for studies which may be prosecuted entirely
in evening classes. The institution of the Faculty was, of course, a direct
outcome of the purpose implicit in the mind of John Owens : and the
manner of dealing with it admirably illustrates the Manchester academic
way : when it has consolidated the strictly academic bases, established
the credentials of its scholarship and of the degrees which are the reward
of it, it is then free to experiment with adaptations to meet the needs of
what Whitehead calls the " insistent present ".

It is, however, in another way that evening classes as they now
exist have most enriched the Owens tradition. The two first principals
of Owens, Scott and Greenwood, had been keenly interested in Working
Men's Colleges, and Owens College never lost the consciousness of its
duty to the people : it had, in due course, its Settlement, and its Extension
lectures ; in the 1890's, indeed, the women students were helping to run
a club for mill girls in Grosvenor Street. But its extra-mural activities
only acquired full Mancunian form and quality after the University secured
its independence. The instrument of it in the first place was H. Pilkington
Turner who with the zeal of a lay-missioner threw himself into the extra-
mural campaign in the direction to which it had recently turned by the
formation of the Workers' Educational Association. In more recent
times, the trend of social thought and of legislation has thrown more and
more emphasis on a university's extra-mural responsibilities : and now
our Extra-Mural Department is fully integrated internally with the
University, has a professor at its head, is a participant in the Faculty of

Education, and not only provides the services which extra-muralities require, lectures, classes, a resident college, etc., but also submits the principles of extra-mural teaching to the same disciplined study as is given to other academic subjects. By and large, it provides a magnificent illustration of the way in which John Owens' injunction to serve the people of his province is being honoured and being honoured in a way which enlarges and enriches the central academic idea itself.

But to return to the committee's report to their fellow-Trustees. They recommended that the college should have six professors at the outset, of whom three would be full-time professors, and would be paid £350 a year. The three full-time professors were to deal respectively with the following groups of subjects (1) Languages and Literature of Greece and Rome; (2) Mathematics and Natural Philosophy; (3) Logic and Mental Philosophy, together with general Grammar and English Language and Literature. It is a gratifying thought to me, especially in these days when the response to literature seems to be taken by our prominent æsthetes as something restricted to sensuous or emotional responses to rhythms and arabesques, that the University in which I have expounded literature for a lifetime saw from its beginnings that there was a real and fundamental connection between logic, philosophy, and literature. Three other chairs were to be established, at £150 a year, since they were part-time appointments. They were to comprise (4) History and Moral and Political Philosophy; (5) Natural History including Botany and Geology, and (6) Chemistry. It was recommended that one of the professors should be appointed as principal of the college and receive an additional £200 a year. The Principal should be given large discretionary power: the committee would seek an " experienced person and define his duties as little as possible ", believing that " he will soon, if he is conscientious, define them for himself, and what he (the first Principal) defines and practices for himself, will become a precedent for his successors ". Moreover, although, at the outset it would be the duty of the Trustees to take full part in devising the initial schemes for the college, once the professors were appointed it was urged on their fellow-Trustees by the committee, that " this being once done there should be no interference by the Trustees with the functions of the Principal and other professors, except on occasions of positive necessity "—a very liberal doctrine of academic government which has prevailed generally through the history of Manchester University. Indeed, the whole attitude of mind of this committee of Trustees and of the Trustees themselves set the pattern for a new type of academic government which, of necessity, had first to be worked out by and for Owens College. The college, it cannot be too often insisted, was the idea of the lay and unacademic mind of Manchester. Its nature and its manner were determined by the opinion prevailing amongst men with such minds. Consequently the man of commerce and industry has always had a large part in the determination of policy : and, as time went along, a constitution emerged in which the lay and the academic teaching members of the college each contributed their appropriate shares in a harmonious and eminently successful partnership. Until 1870, the Trustees were the sole governors of the college ; they appointed the teaching staff and received reports from them on work done. As we have just seen, however, they proclaimed at the outset their intention not to interfere with the academic functions of the staff " except on reasons of positive necessity ". They kept their word. In due course, as the college grew, a less personal design in government seemed called for. By the parliamentary act of 1870, the private trust was abolished, and the college incorporated : it was provided with a con- stitution, comprising President, Court, Council and Senate. The Council was the executive committee of the large and widely representative Court : Council was, in fact, the effective governing body of the college, but it left all strictly academic matters to Senate. Naturally just what is strictly academic and whether any university matter can be said to be independent of the financial and other material implications of its operation, are fine points for argument. By the experience of the years, however, and above all, by the sympathetic allowances made by both sides, the scheme has worked extremely well. It has enabled the University to keep closely integrated with its region ; it has brought the invigoratingly fresh breeze of lay opinion when, as sometimes happens, the academic mind sequesters itself in Utopian policies ; it has brought the practical sympathy of men whose wealth enabled them to be generous benefactors : but above all, it has brought the goodwill, the wisdom, and the untiring day-to-day interest of some of the finest of Manchester's and Lancashire's character- istic people. Their names are legion, but one thinks particularly of Thomas Ashton, of Edward Donner, of Arthur Worthington and of Christopher Needham.

Perhaps only at one point has the progressive harmony between Council and Senate been really seriously threatened. By the 1870 Act,

Council is empowered " to appoint the principal and professors, and make contracts with them, and before proceeding to the election of a professor the council shall in ordinary cases advertise for and receive candidates' applications and testimonials, and shall refer the same to the Senate for examination, arrangement, and report : *but the Council shall not be obliged to adopt the report or be bound by the recommendation of the Senate.*" The habitual practice up to 1903 appears to have been for Senate to put names of those thought worthy in order of merit ; and Council seems to have then interviewed those at the top of the list, and made their choice. It is said that once, and once only, they chose a professor whose name had not been on the Senate's list of recommendations. And, if the rumour is true, the choice completely justified the Council. But when in 1903 Manchester became an independent university, Senate was more and more realising that on the whole the choice of a professor was perhaps the most important factor in the University's endeavour to establish and maintain the highest standards of scholarship : and Senate felt, that as the matter at issue was scholarship, Senate was the proper judge. There is no record that there was a set debate or a particular conflict on the point. But it is evident that there was skirmishing. In 1904 Senate asked Council to interview two chosen candidates for a chair, but only, apparently, because they, Senate, were divided between the two. In the same year, Council suggested that applications for the Engineering Chair should be first considered by a joint-committee of Council and Senate. Senate declined, and set up their own recommending committee. It is a right which it has maintained up to the present day. Council for many years still insisted on interviewing Senate's nominees. Probably the last time it did so formally was in 1913, and as in that year it issued an instruction that for elections to chairs, testimonials of all candidates thought worthy of consideration should be circulated to Council, it may be it was finally convinced that Senate is indeed the body to choose professors. Senate certainly does it with scrupulous care. It sets up a sub-committee : extensive enquiries are made from all appropriate people and places : the committee scrutinises all the information made available, and interviews the people in whom it is interested. The virtue of the Manchester way of doing it is this, that whilst all outside experts are consulted, the selecting committee is entirely a committee of the Manchester Senate ; for, in his character as a man, the incoming professor must somehow fit into the organism which is Manchester University. In my time at Manchester, Council has always appointed the person chosen by Senate.

Perhaps another reason which has added greatly to the efficiency and the smoothness of Manchester University's government is both fortuitous and deliberate. In the choice of officers like Vice-Chancellors, Registrars and Bursars, who are the daily link between Council and Senate, and the interpreters of one body to the other, Manchester has been incredibly fortunate in finding men who however they may have differed in what may be called the techniques of their post, however varied in their success as vice-chancellors or registrars or bursars, have nevertheless been the kind of human being who generally by nature, though in a few cases only by acquirement, is master of the art of getting on with folks.

Hence, in 1951, in still another aspect of the corporate life of the University, we see how what we are is the natural unfolding of the original Owens idea as it was first interpreted by his first Trustees. The report they issued in 1850, in general and in detail, is a characteristic statement of the breadth and the foresight of the liberal mind of Manchester when it directed itself to those intellectual, social, moral, and political problems which converge in the philosophy and in the practice of higher education. The attitude of mind pervading the report is succinctly implicit in its final paragraphs. " It cannot but be felt that the first scheme, however carefully prepared, must be regarded as experimental, and that it may be found necessary after an adequate trial to modify it in a greater or less degree. . . . Every establishment for education, securing certain fundamental matters, should have a latitude so as to conform to what experience may prove to be desirable." " The scheme should be made as general as possible . . . so that the scheme may possess the capability of adaptation to what may be found to be the wants of the community." This last clause is another witness of the intuitive wisdom of these representative Manchester non-academic men who were shaping a college which became a university. Their plan for elasticity and generality so that the " wants of the community " may be a permanent criterion (they had already safeguarded the traditionally academic core) has been one of the most vital directives in the history of the University. It became the law of Manchester's progressive principle : it was the motive which instigated research in the sciences and in medicine : it was the motive which prompted expansion of traditional subjects into new fields, as, for instance, it instigated the historians to break into the new historical field of economic history; it is still the same motive which, realising that the traditional arts subjects may find it more and more difficult to maintain their impact on modern civilisation, is resulting in an extensive development of those social sciences in which science and arts (always an abstract distinction) are becoming more and more indissolubly united than they have been since their formal divorce centuries ago. These Owens Trustees of 1850 would have been gratified could they have known how closely their notions were working towards the principles of what should distinguish university work, as such principles were enunciated more than three-quarters of a century later by the great mathematician, scholar and philosopher, Whitehead, in 1932. By the Trustees' emphasis on responsiveness to the pressure of time, place and circumstance, they were providing a safeguard against the congenital academic danger of a pleasant existence in an intellectual world of inert ideas. They were taking for granted that a useless education is a foolish contradiction of mere words. Education, they felt, was an art which taught how to make use of knowledge; and knowledge, if it is to be used, must be used in the present, that is, by those who use it and in the environment in which its use is beneficial. It is impossible to live, materially or spiritually, unless one can deal with the insistent present, either by blanketing oneself against it as the pedant does, or by seeking to meet it as John Owens and his Trustees sought to do. They were not in the least advocates of a merely technical education. They wanted the college to seek for and propound the science behind the practical arts, and to explore the practically artistic applications of science. They had an intuitive sense of the power of knowledge, and were beginning to realise the immense power of ideas. They divined how this sense of the power of knowledge could be imparted to students through the particular bodies of knowledge which have direct reference to their own daily lives; they grasped therefore that for these students, typical Manchester students, the proper higher education was to inculcate a sense of the significance and power of ideas by leading them to see the ideas which lay behind what in day to day life they recognised as the efficient and even profitable practical arts. Once the intellectual union between effective practice and sound theory had been made in the student's mind, then one major objective of education had been attained, the adventure of action had been linked with the greater adventure of thought. The Trustees had not, perhaps, an intuitive perception of what Whitehead calls the beauty of ideas ; but their basic plans would lead their disciples to a perception of these in due course.

The report to the Trustees adverted to one other topic of paramount importance in the mind of the Founder, one which was time and again re-called in the history of his foundation.   John Owens and all the liberals amongst his acquaintances whom he named as Trustees were devoutly religious men.   But whether Unitarians, or Congregationalists or Wesleyans, almost all of them were nonconformists : and no nonconformist could qualify for a degree at Oxford or Cambridge.   Perhaps in the complex of John Owens' reaction to such a situation, there was something of the sentiments which Kingsley was to express in 1850 as Parson Lot, in an article in *The Christian Socialist* on " The Opening of the Universities to the People ", and more fervently in his novel *Alton Locke* of the same year.   A passionate radical character in the story, old Mackaye, is pointing out by whose injustice university education is kept beyond the reach of men like the hero of the novel, men of the working and lower middle class.   " Why, the parsons' injustice to be sure.   They've got the monopoly of education in England, and they get their bread by it at their public schools and universities, and of course it's their interest to keep up the price of their commodity, and let no man have a taste of it who can't pay down handsomely.   And so those aristocrats of college dons go on rolling in riches, and fellowships and scholarships that were bequeathed by the people's friends in old times just to educate poor scholars like you and me and give us our rights as free men."   John Owens would doubtless have disowned some of Kingsley's political views, but, though of different religious persuasions, both were unswervingly religious in their beliefs.   John Owens' governing motive in founding his college has frequently been confused by an imperfect analogy with the founding of University College, London, in 1826.   It would be unfair to see a foundation so closely linked with Bentham as part of a deliberate trend towards secularism, but it is clear that some of the most active supporters of the foundation were held by their contemporaries in the counterpart, or counterblast, King's College, to be " infidels ".   Owens College, however, was not meant to be, and most emphatically was not, a secularist foundation.   There was not amongst its first Trustees a single person who, even in the suspicious nomenclature of the day, could have been called a freethinker.   They were all openly, and most of them strongly, attached to one or other of the recognised religious communities.   What John Owens had done was to preclude any sectarian exclusiveness. All sects were to be admitted and therefore there were to be no religious tests whatever. There was to be freedom of thinking, but there was no bias whatever to prefer nor to provide for the so-called " free-thinkers ".

The first of the " immutable conditions " which governed the college not only prohibited religious tests, but also laid down that nothing in the teaching of the college should be offensive to the conscience of its members and of the community of its friends. Hence at once arose the question as to how far anything relating to religion should be recognised as an official activity of the college. The Trustees, having devoted the attention due to such an important problem, recommended that " religious instruction should be provided for all the students who may desire to avail themselves of it, and that such instruction should be given by the Principal or by one of the other professors ". Attendance, however, was to be entirely optional. In that way the Trustees hoped that, " such religious instruction as may elevate and strengthen the moral and religious character of the students, without encroaching on the liberty of conscience " would be available. Oddly enough, when their report was publicly available, objections to their intention to include even so much, or so little, religious teaching arose in the very circles which had been John Owens' earlier religious environment, the nonconformist community. Unitarians, Presbyterians and Congregationalists made formal representation to the Trustees against the proposal, even though it was made clear that the religious instruction would be optional, and would concern itself only with the evidences of Christianity and the foundations of natural and revealed religion. On the other side, a deputation of Anglicans approved the proposal. But that in itself was likely, and not without reason, to arouse the suspicion of many Manchester liberals : and the *Manchester Guardian* gave its columns to the expression of the opinions of those who feared that in practice it would be impossible to safeguard sincere religious instruction from the sectarian bias of the person who gave it. In effect, the religious instruction which was eventually provided was no more than what would to-day be regarded as a normal and a proper part of the academic activities of any university body, the study of the New Testament in Greek, of the Old Testament in Hebrew, and a course of public lectures by the Principal on " The Influence of Religion in relation to the Life of the Scholar ". It is a long cry from this to the institution of a Faculty of Theology as an integral part of the comprehensive range of knowledge by which a university distinguishes itself from an academic college. It was not, in fact, until 1903, that the Faculty was established. However, there were many, and those not merely obstructionist difficulties, to overcome before that consummation was achieved. One of them lay in the deep-seated suspicion of even the slightest appearance of sectarian preference, for it was as an enfranchisement from the penalties of sectarian preference that Owens College had been born. Throughout the century, in the whole field of public education, feeling between the sects seemed again and again to frustrate the progress of educational policy. The Council of Owens College, in 1875, soon after it succeeded to the governing powers formerly exercised by the Trustees, was soon confronted with a situation which illustrates the intense nervousness about anything which might arouse sectarian animosities. R. D. Darbishire, a Trustee, afterwards Life-Governor and member of the Council, and in due course one of the three residuary legatees of Sir Joseph Whitworth, one of our most munificent benefactors, drew attention to the money given to the college by his brother in 1874 for the purchase of books on condition that some of the books bought out of the fund should be "so-called sacred books and works on comparative theology, but not such as treat of dogmatic or controversial subjects in a spirit other than that of scientific and unprejudiced pursuit of truth". Mr. Darbishire proposed to Council that the purpose prompting the gift would be carried considerably further forward if the college instituted a series of weekly sermons to be given by chosen representatives of the different sects. But the Senate, a body of men of deep religious sentiments, reported against the plan because "public feeling on the question of a comprehensive system of religious and moral instruction which shall command the adhesion of the great majority, and yet offend the just susceptibilities of none" is as yet unprepared for such a plan. They feared that the college might be accused of departing from the Founder's fundamental and immutable condition, the avoidance of offence to any man's conscience.

The principle involved was indeed fundamental to the Manchester way of thought. As the years went on, and as sectarian feeling became less exacerbated, a less negative compromise was possible. Sir Alfred Hopkinson tells how a similar difficulty was dealt with in 1902 when the college was arranging the celebration of its jubilee. A commemoration service in the Cathedral was suggested. There was opposition; it was countered formally by arranging for the Dean to issue the initial invitation to governors and members of the college to attend a commemoration service in the Cathedral where the Bishop would preach the sermon. There was still opposition, but it was largely assuaged by another of Sir Alfred's expedients. Before the arrangements for the Cathedral service were made publicly known, Dr. Alexander Maclaren, the most distinguished and effective nonconformist preacher in Manchester, had been with some difficulty persuaded to preach in his own church to members of the University on the Sunday following the Cathedral service ; and the two services were first announced publicly in the same notice.

It has already been pointed out how the establishment of a Founder's Day Ceremony was for long held up by uncertainty about the association of it with a specifically religious ceremony. One remembers, too, that when the Faculty of Theology in 1924 sought Senate's approval for a course of lectures on St. Thomas Aquinas to be given by a great Catholic authority on the subject, Father Bede Jarrett, it had already been arranged that that stalwart Anglican, Tout, should deliver the introductory lecture to the course ; and, giving its approval to the arrangement, Senate reminded the promoters to be mindful of the conditions of the Founder's Will. Even as recently as the late 'thirties, one recalls the concern of some of the wisest and most senior members of Senate, when, by oversight, a particular Sunday was described in the official *University Pocket Diary* as the day on which the "University Sermon" would be preached. The spirit of John Owens persists. There is still no University Sermon officially sanctioned by the University. We still hold to the faith that truth is more likely to emerge from the collision of many doctrines than from the institutional predominance of any one.

But it must be again insisted that these characteristic manifestations were not expressions of hostility to religion. They were safeguards against sectarian preference. They were points of view inherent in the college as a Manchester organism. How essentially religious the prevailing atmosphere was at the outset is made clear when one glances at the interests of the men whom the Trustees appointed as the first professors of the college, and notes how, in their lectures, the professors' religious beliefs became, not only incidentally, but even glaringly, apparent.

The first Principal, A. J. Scott, was a son of the manse, himself brought up for the ministry of the Presbyterian Church, fervently religious, immersed in doctrinal problems, and even after these speculative questions

had led to his withdrawal from the Presbyterian Church, he continued to
preach in his little chapel in Woolwich until he was appointed professor
of English Language and Literature in University College, London. He
came to Manchester as Principal and Professor in 1851. It fell to him to
give the course of lectures the institution of which had seemed to some of
Manchester's public to be contrary to the non-sectarian conditions imposed
by the Founder. He chose as his topic *The Influence of Religion in relation
to the Life of the Scholar*, and the whole trend of his argument was deeply
religious. Greenwood, appointed in 1851 as first professor of the
Languages and Literatures of Greece and Rome, and successor to Scott as
Principal in 1857, instilled into pupils and public alike the doctrine that
" the only lawful aim in the desire after learning and knowledge is to seek
in knowledge a rich storehouse for the glory of the Creator and the relief
of man's estate ". The first professor of Mathematics, Sandeman,
concluded a highly philosophic survey of the nature of mathematical
studies with this exordium—" as certainly as we live, so certainly must
we philosophise ; that it is death with us, in all but mere bodily sense,
when we cease to have appetite for enquiry : that, in short, ' Man doth not
live by bread alone but by every word that proceedeth out of the mouth
of God '." In Sandeman's remark, there is something of vital importance
to the future of Owens, quite apart from the bearing of the quotation on
the topic for which it was quoted. Sandeman was not a successful
teacher ; but neither he nor his colleagues knew, in those years, whether
they were schoolmasters or professors, for the age of permissible entry to
Owens College was fourteen. Sandeman was always above the heads
of his class ; and in 1865, after fourteen years' tenure as first professor of
Mathematics, he retired to the much more lucrative responsibility of
managing the family's jute works in Dundee. But though he had not
been successful as a teacher of mathematics, he had been a perpetual
stimulus to a non-mathematical and more important quality in his students'
intellectual experience : he had impressed on them the primary law of
real living, the incessant " appetite for enquiry ".

Williamson, the first professor of Natural History, claimed that his
subject was " one of the handmaids to Revelation ". Perpetually observ-
ing the world of nature about him, a naturalist's " heart must, indeed, be
insensible, and the moral feelings blunted, in which emotions thus excited,
do not sometimes ascend to Him who clothes the lilies of the field and
feeds the young ravens when they cry ". He turns aside to rebuke those

A. W. WARD, Principal 1885–1897
(*From the portrait by H. von Herkomer*)

of " that Pantheistic philosophy which would put an imaginary power, called Nature, in the place of God, rob Him of his personality, and thus depose Him from the throne of His own universe ". What men call " nature's laws are but the self-imposed rules by which the Creator has chosen to regulate His own creative acts ". The first Professor of Chemistry, Frankland, introduced his subject by pointing out how much less its discoveries have been used than have those of other sciences ; yet " the position which Chemistry now occupies amongst the sciences is a most elevated and honourable one ", and, in the first place, it holds this position because it " exemplifies the wisdom and goodness of the great Creator in the transcendently beautiful, perfect, and harmonious laws which He has impressed upon matter ".

A Senate of men holding in common a basis of belief such as the one expressed in the above quotations is not likely to build up an irreligious or an anti-religious community. Their unswerving orthodoxy on the major articles of faith is all the more remarkable in that the scientists amongst them are most specific in their display of it : and that, too, in 1850, when the Victorian conflict between science and religion was already joined, though its major battles were to be deferred for a few years.

Such was Owens College when it started. How far were the ideals which brought it into existence capable of energising it as a living organism which progressively would realise and extend its immediate purpose, an organism which, through the continual impact between itself and the circumstances of its nearer and remoter environment, would discover, as if by its own instinct, functions hitherto dormant yet inherent in its own nature ? How far will its history down to 1951 justify the wisdom of Owens' intentions, and how will the record show the University's fidelity as Trustee of Owens' foundation ? The answer is scarcely open to doubt. The University to-day is simply the Owens' idea growing in the way of its own nature to a larger and larger life. It is still essentially faithful to the fundamental purpose of its Founder. Growth demands modification, adaptations, and changes which may on the surface seem large. But even these changes which seem drastic to the eye are not really the discarding of a limb nor the removal of an organ from the body which John Owens projected. They are often departures from the letter, the better to realise the spirit. Examples of this, in particular, are the admission to the college of women students, the setting up of a Faculty of Theology, and the provision of facilities for residential as distinct from day-students.

But in none of these is there a departure from a clear conviction of the Founder, though there may here and there seem a disparity between the legal and the implicit meaning of his testamentary phrase.

Take, for instance, the admission of women to the rights of the University equally with men. This was one of the most outstanding events in the unfolding of the inherent idea of Manchester University. It was an event for which non-Mancunians have hailed Manchester as a pioneer in academic history. But the history of its coming about is very characteristically Mancunian, characteristic of the exquisite balance between the thrust to futher progress and the determination to safeguard the past. The admission of women, for instance, was no sympathetic gesture to a rampant feminist movement. In the days of the suffragette movement, Sylvia Pankhurst was a student here ; and she was properly summoned to appear before the Discipline Committee of the University after she had been fined at the Police Court for disorderly behaviour. The admission of women to Manchester University was a natural consequence of what Manchester reason took to be common human justice. Roscoe, one of the most effective shapers of our academic tradition, contributed an article to the college magazine for May, 1870, on the education of women. In the article he was particularly concerned to put the proposition that, not only were women entitled to a general cultural and academic education, but that they were also entitled to the other, and the increasingly more significant, sort of university education which qualifies the student to practise one of the various professions. Roscoe was enthusiastically in favour of opening these professions to women. " Are we to open the liberal professions (as they are, perhaps, sarcastically termed) to women, or not ? If women with us are not to be allowed to practise as surgeons or physicians or to dispense justice as in Wyoming or medicines as in France, they need not trouble themselves about any professional training, but may devote themselves to obtaining that general elevation of feeling and character which a higher intellectual position must necessarily secure to them. For my own part (Roscoe goes on) I can see no reason why women should be debarred by legal or social enactment from taking any position to which their powers or talents entitle them. I believe that the principles of free-trade hold good in intellectual as well as in commercial affairs." So, Roscoe said, he would welcome women in all his classes.

The year in which Roscoe wrote this, 1870, was the year in which, by a legal device, or as legal purists said, by legal subterfuge, parliamentary action was in process of enabling Owens College to amalgamate itself as The Owens College with an Owens Extension College to which no legal prohibition of women students was attached. But although the legal procedure to achieve the desired end was stigmatised as sharp practice by the puritans at law, there can be no doubt that, in securing legal admission to admit women to the college, the authorities were transcending the letter to achieve the spirit of John Owens' endowment. There is not the slightest doubt that the words of John Owens' will do limit the use of his bounty to the education of the male sex, " to found an institution for providing or aiding the means of instructing and improving young persons of the male sex ". But that, taken in its setting in time and circumstance, does not imply a rooted objection to the use of it for the education of women. It is rather a matter of priorities in what the resources of his endowment could provide. There is a corroborative parallel in a provision of the will which regulates priorities in the admission of men. There can be no questioning of the fixedness of John Owens' intention to make his college a place which, in the first instance, would serve the needs of the city or county or region in which it was to be established. The second of the " two fundamental and immutable rules and conditions " which he laid down for the use of his bounty was this : " if, and as often as the number of applicants for admission to such an institution as students, shall be more than adequate to the means of the institution, a preference shall *in all cases* be given to the children of parents residing . . . within the limits now comprised within the parliamentary borough of Manchester or within two miles from any part of such limits ; and *secondly*, to the children of parents residing . . . within the limits comprised in the parliamentary district or division of South Lancashire : *but subject as aforesaid, the said institution shall be open to all applicants for admission, without respect to place of birth and without distinction of rank or condition in society* ". There at least is a clear revelation of the Founder's idea. He would like to educate Lancashire ; he knew that his legacy could only do a part of what he wished to do, and so, he chose to educate Manchester first, Lancashire second, and then, if resources would reach to it, he would admit anybody who was thought fit to be admitted. Knowing the wide need for education, knowing, too, that his bounty could only provide for a relatively small response to the total need, he had to indicate such priorities. Without any feeling whatever about the education of women, he would inevitably be first conscious of the

immediate need for the higher education of men.   Indeed, although in the
very year in which he made his will, Charlotte Brontë was staying in the
house of Mrs. Gaskell which was only a short walk from John Owens'
house, there is no reason to think that the question of the education of
women, as an urgent social problem, had entered his head.   His restriction of the scope of his college to the education of men was automatic
rather than deliberate, the result of circumstance rather than of personal
conviction or of personal prejudice or whim.   Attempts by others living
later to explain an exclusion which needs no explanation turn to the fact
that he was a bachelor, and therefore it is easily assumed that he was a
misogynist.   Fiddes exposes the flimsiness of this reconstruction of John
Owens' personality.   He was no more a misogynist than a misanthropist.
Of course, when the terms of the will are interpreted, as they must be,
in a strictly legal sense, no part of the endowment can be applied to the
education of women.   But the legal prohibition was circumvented
properly by a legal device : indeed, it proved less of an obstacle than was
the natural hardening of the liberal minds of the authorities as they grew
older.   When the rights of entry for women had been legally secured in
1871, it took twelve more years before Principal Greenwood could be
moved to implement that right.

The whole story of the admission of women to Manchester University
is one of the most significant chapters in its history.   It has been told at
length by a Manchester graduate, Mrs. Mabel Tylecote, in a volume
published by the University Press in 1941.   To that volume Edward Fiddes
contributed a foreword, and, on a centenary occasion, the words of Fiddes
on such a significant chapter in the development of our tradition are
worthy of reprinting.   They are reprinted here in an appendix.

The long struggle to establish a department or a Faculty of Theology
was not in effect brought about by legal difficulty.   As was strenuously
asserted by Sir Alfred Hopkinson, our Professor of Jurisprudence and
Law from 1875 to 1890, our Principal from 1898 to 1913, and, in the
meantime, Vice-Chancellor of the Victoria University for his appointed
period, and ultimately Vice-Chancellor of Manchester University from
1904 to 1913, John Owens' will did not forbid, as it had erroneously been
taken to forbid, the teaching of religious subjects.   The major trouble
was that in the days of the federal Victoria University, from 1880 to 1903,
two of the constituent colleges, for different reasons, were hostile to the
establishment of religious and theological pursuits within the university.

Liverpool was legally prohibited from the inclusion of religious teaching in any form, and Leeds was antipathetic because it feared that the university ideal of secular truth would be distorted by the variant forms of theological truth. Manchester, however, had seen how an adaptation of the Owens' idea might meet the situation. As a college devoted to the study of and the search for truth, as a foundation devoted to such subjects as are or may be taught in universities, its founder imposed on it an obligation to teach a subject so traditional as was theology. Moreover, as subjects like philosophy, history, and literature were included in the normal curriculum, it was obvious that the innumerable repercussions of such subjects, merely in their normal academic implications, would require an academic representation of the study of theology. Sir Adolphus Ward, during his Principalship, was energetic in the endeavour to establish theology as an academic subject ; so, too, was Sir Alfred Hopkinson who succeeded him, and, whilst Ward was a practising and convinced Anglican, Hopkinson had been brought up as a devout nonconformist. However, whilst the University was a federal one, neither Ward nor Hopkinson could establish in Owens a real department of theology, even though there was another aspect of the Owens' idea which had made Ward particularly anxious to have a theological department established. Owens desired to serve the needs of the vicinity : Ward was convinced that one of those needs was the college's participation in the training of ministers and parsons, training not only in their preliminary secular subjects but in their theological studies. When the University became free, it at once (1903) set up a Faculty of Theology, and doing so, it exemplified and developed still another of the ideas in the Owens scheme. Just as the incorporation of the Medical School had related the University as such to already established institutions for the study and practice of medicine, and had employed, in a part-time capacity, men whose main occupation was in the hospitals, so the setting up of the Faculty of Theology brought into direct relationship with the University the many sectarian colleges situated in or near to Manchester. As the Faculty now operates, and as it was meant to operate, the bulk of the theological teaching is in the University and is given by full-time University teachers ; but where matters of sectarian doctrine are concerned, the teaching is in the sectarian college, though a theological student of any other sect may attend. Moreover, some of the theological college teachers are recognised as university teachers and give their lectures in the University. John Owens would have applauded the outcome of his project, would have felt that the University was still free from all sectarian preference, since, in a way he could not at his time have foreseen, it had devised a means of comprising in its curriculum the whole range of traditional theological studies.   In 1851 and down to 1900, how-ever, the time was not ripe.   Until there arose in preachers and theologians a frame of mind which was swayed less by sectarian differences in doctrine than by a desire to explore the common grounds on which all might co-operate without violating the sanctity of their own private beliefs, there could be no reasonably comprehensive Faculty of Theology.   More-over, a community which arises from and lives in the intellectual atmo-sphere which was characteristic of Owens College in its first fifty years would feel acutely the necessity of safeguarding against such violation. But its insistence on the sanctity of conscience was ultimately only one aspect of its devotion to freedom of thought ; and its liberalism engendered a social conscience which would at length compel it to recognise the necessity of co-operation in order to secure a common good.   A Faculty of Theology was inevitable.

The extension of facilities to allow a larger and larger proportion of the students the opportunity to be residential, instead of day-students, a trend in the policy of the University which has latterly been more and more powerfully supported, is a feature which appears a more apparent divergence from any scheme which John Owens could have imagined than does any other development.   John Owens had in mind, first of all, the youth of Manchester, youth, too, as young as fourteen.   He wanted to reduce the costs of a liberal general education to the lowest necessary amount.   He shared with his fellow-nonconformists a belief that religious and moral training was best strengthened within the home and the family. It is hardly likely, therefore, that the notion of endowing a residential college would have ever forced itself into his mind as a major problem ; and if it had done so, he would probably have been reluctant to deprive young students of the advantage of living in their family circle.   He may even have heard, too, from some of his acquaintances who were familiar with the history of the famous nonconformist Warrington Academy that its ultimate failure had been set down, not so much to lack of resources, but to difficulties it had brought on to itself by its residential scheme.   It is not without interest to notice the opinion which the first Vice-Chancellor of Manchester University, Sir Alfred Hopkinson, set down towards the end of his life in *Penultima* (1930).   The book is largely occupied with educational topics, since for almost the whole of his life he had been associated with educational work. He summarily records this as his opinion on boarding-schools : " In spite of some obvious advantages in the boarding school system, I am disposed to think as the result of subsequent experience that for many families, especially where there are more than two or three children, the day school is often the best, at all events where the parents have character and sufficient leisure to enable them to throw themselves into the life and the interests of their sons and daughters." It is a sentiment nearer to that of John Owens than to the one which was becoming more prevalent amongst the Manchester men who were the sons of families like the Hopkinsons, and to whom Rugby, Winchester, and Eton began to mean something very different from what Owens and Manchester University had felt to be urgent in education.

But as Owens College grew and the range of area from which its students came extended itself more and more widely, the problem passed from the realm of doctrine into that of immediate necessity. Students had to find shelter and board. The earlier Manchester man would have recollected how a similar situation was met in the Scottish universities : the students from country districts lived sparely and arduously in meagre attic lodgings. But perhaps Manchester was becoming too liberal to contemplate such rigours as a necessary discipline in austerity or as an entirely successful way of inculcating the necessity of hard work. At all events, there could be no suggestion that the Founder's will could be cited as a legal prohibition of Halls of Residence. It did, of course, limit the proportion of the Trust Fund which could be spent on buildings ; but it recognised as primary charges on the fund the provision for students of such " aids, assistance and encouragement " as were necessary for the promotion of their studies. It cited especially the providing of " books and other requisites for such studies " and empowered the trustees to furnish all other means to the same end as they " shall in their absolute discretion think fit ". Even in 1857, when the six-year-old college seemed likely to collapse through lack of students, the academic staff reported that one, though a subsidiary, cause was the absence of any sort of residential arrangement which would enable them to instil a pattern of academic discipline into the students. They were thinking, obviously, in terms of a school rather than of a college which was to become a university. But the college recovered, and it recovered by increasing the power of its own intellectual organism instead of by resorting to more peripheral devices. Still, when, in due course, the problem of housing students had become considerable, and suggestions were made by independent authorities to establish and maintain hostels for students, the idea was approved. The promoters of these ventures were, as one would expect, religious bodies, who, whether Anglican or nonconformist, were familiar with the use of hostels for their own sectarian training purposes. The first attempt to establish such a hostel was made as early as 1870, when a Church of England Hall of Residence was set up in Plymouth Grove, although at that time the college was still in Quay Street, down in the middle of the city. The project, however, soon failed through lack of funds, and because of a certain native antipathy to Anglican priority. The Quakers were more successful. They seized the propitious moment when the college was moving from Quay Street to its present home and converted three houses, not too distant from the new site, into the Friends' Hall which was opened in 1876, and was transferred, re-named as Dalton Hall, to Victoria Park in 1882. The Anglican Hulme Hall followed in 1887. The problem was vastly intensified when women were admitted to the University. Again, it was as a private undertaking that the provision of a hall was organised. But on this occasion the organising body was a group of men of various religious beliefs, met together in an entirely non-sectarian capacity, as friends of the University and of the higher education of women, men like C. P. Scott, R. D. Darbishire, and Samuel Alexander. Their scheme, however, did allot to the University as such a direct share in the government of the proposed hall, a rôle destined to become more and more significant until virtually, and then in fact, Ashburne Hall became not a licensed Hall of Residence but a University Hall of Residence. It had begun in Victoria Park in 1900, in 1908 it had moved to its present site in Fallowfield, and on this it has grown to larger and larger capacity. Its Anglican counterpart began as the Victoria Church Hostel in 1904 and was transferred to Victoria Park and re-named Langdale Hall in 1911. Both this and St. Anselm Hall for men students were projects initiated by Bishop Knox when he came to the Manchester See in 1903 : and though St. Anselm, being at first a hostel for Anglican ordinands, was not officially recognised by the University, in due course (1920) it became, like the rest of the men's hostels, a " licensed " Hall of Residence. The circumstances which make such licensed halls a necessity, and the frame of mind which puts high value on the corporate sense they often inculcate, have gained in their force ;

rightly organised, they can, and must, safeguard themselves against depriving a student of the sacred right of privacy, since in the last resort, it is in the private recesses of his own mind and his own soul that his conquest is to be won. Since St. Anselm other existing fraternities have been recognised as licensed halls ; for example, Lancashire Independent College (1922) and the Unitarian College (1927). For the women students, Ashburne has gone on growing, generally by exercising a suzerainty over temporary outlying houses and then absorbing them into her own campus by an extension of its buildings. So Ward Hall was opened as a temporary expedient in 1919 and was in 1925 taken into Ashburne as its Ward Wing. Lees Hall was another outlying territory, set up in 1919, and in 1932 incorporated in the Lees Wing at Ashburne. At present there is a further Ashburne development on the edge of the campus. The Stopford Wing (1946), except for a short distance in space, is otherwise an integral part of Ashburne. Moreover, one other women's hall has been established with the same relationship to the University as has Ashburne, that is, a body, not merely licensed, but governed by a univerity delegacy, namely the Ellis Llwyd Jones Hall, established by benefaction in 1919. The other newer women's hall is a licensed hall, St. Gabriel's, the home of many of our Roman Catholic women students since 1921. Lister House is a special hostel for the residence of medical students for a short compulsory period during their clinical training ; established in 1911, it was a novel departure in Redbrick Medical Schools, a pioneering venture which had to be closed in 1914 owing to the exigences of war, but was re-established in 1934 and has succeeded even beyond expectation.

The progress and expanse of this residential feature of the University's activities has throughout been very critically watched by many academic members of the University's government. Manchester could not be allowed to become a series of colleges which with independent authority would obstruct the necessary autonomy of a young university. The James Heywood, previously mentioned as an original trustee of Owens College and as a campaigner in parliament for the reform of Oxford and Cambridge (he himself had been a student at Cambridge), was not only anxious to rid them of religious tests ; he was eager to save the University from the tyranny of its colleges. The ultimate loyalties of Manchester's residential students must be to their University, and not to their Hall. One has sometimes felt that, through the mere increase of the Manchester staff and the consequent growth of the bulk and weight of Oxford and

Cambridge opinion within it, the function of a Manchester Hall of Residence was liable to be confused with that of an Oxford or Cambridge college. But the Manchester policy has the weight of wide educational authority behind it; and even if one somewhat questions the efficiency of lodging arrangements to produce a " social " sense, and questions even more the value of such social capacity as they may seem to foster, there is no doubt that the halls do provide a *milieu* well-suited to encourage the proper activities of a university student.

Their provision is, in fact, a further instance illustrative of the way the University has been faithful to Owens' trust. It is a particular example of the exercise of the obligation as interpreted by the Trustees themselves when they planned the college. " Every establishment for education, securing certain fundamental matters, should have a latitude so as to conform to what experience may prove to be desirable ", so that its " scheme may possess the capability of providing what may be found to be the wants of the community ".

CHAPTER IV

COLLEGE TO UNIVERSITY: THE
ROSCOE-WARD EPOCH

OWENS COLLEGE came into being in March, 1851. Its primary object was to make the teaching of traditional university subjects easily accessible to the inhabitants of Manchester and its neighbourhood. From the outset its initiators had the intention of seeking university status for the college as soon as circumstances were propitious. It was, of course, recognised that it would take a considerable time to achieve this. The college easily secured the right to certify that certain of its students, having followed systematic courses for three years, were eligible to compete for degrees of the University of London. London, however, very soon made that right meaningless by opening its degrees to any candidate, whether collegiate or private. It was not until 1880, as the first constituent college of a newly created federal university, the Victoria University, that Owens College attained university status. But this was not complete academic recognition; and it was not until 1903/4 that the full objective, recognition as an independent and autonomous university, was secured. In 1903 the Victoria University shed its constituent colleges, and one of them, the first, Owens College, in 1904 became The Victoria University of Manchester.

From 1851, the college's first task was to demonstrate its fitness to be recognised as a university. To do so, therefore, its primary and most obvious occupation was to teach subjects traditionally recognised as academic. The subjects were traditional; but by John Owens' instruction they were to be taught to a particular clientèle. It is precisely by this particular injunction that the direction of the college's evolution has been determined. In growing to what it had become by 1901, and in progressing from that so spectacularly to what it is in 1951, the vitalising energy, the *élan vital*, has sprung from its specific choice to live in, to

53

live by, and above all, to live for the community to which it belongs. The result is that having secured academic recognition by showing itself capable of providing what contemporary opinion demanded from universities, it went on, still propelled by its original ideal, and became an increasingly powerful impetus in enlarging the nation's idea of the function of a university. It is not merely that it became the example of a method of academic apprenticeship, a trial period in a semi-university condition of partial dependence, not merely that it provided a model for the physical, external as well as the academic-internal design of university colleges, their framework, and their curricula. It is something far more vital. In 1845 John Owens was simply adopting the general British academic view of universities in regarding them primarily and almost exclusively as teaching institutions. But by stressing their obligation to be aware of and to respond to the region which they served, John Owens was setting free a power which would later force on to universities the recognition of their obligation not only to transmit knowledge, but to extend the frontiers of it by investigation. The Manchester region was industrial ; its industrial operations produced scientific problems ; academic science could co-operate in their solution. It was largely through Roscoe, Professor of Chemistry at Owens from 1857 to 1886, that experimental science became the motive force by which the British idea of a university was revolutionised. Investigation by experiment was a general pattern of research which Roscoe had seen in operation in German universities. As a scientific technique, however, it was capable of adaptation to investigations occupied with problems in other fields of knowledge. To Roscoe's impetus on the scientific activities of Owens College, there was soon joined an ideally appropriate co-adjutator on the Arts side, A. W. Ward. Ward knew Germany and its universities even more familiarly than did Roscoe ; he had lived there in boyhood and in adolescence. He knew, too, its academic ways of thought. So, whilst Roscoe was domiciling research as a major function in the academic pursuit of the physical sciences, Ward accepted a similar obligation to pass from a teacher's transmission to a researcher's extension of knowledge in the field of the humanities. But Ward's problem was much more difficult than Roscoe's. The general notion of investigation by experiment suggests itself almost automatically as the inevitable method of scientific research. But the attempt to discover an equivalent technique for the humane studies raises much more complex questions in so far as criteria

ALFRED HOPKINSON, Principal 1898–1904, Vice-Chancellor
of Manchester University, 1904–1913

(*Photograph by Lafayette*)

in some of those subjects involve assessment of values rather than extension of factual information. Ward, however, was in person the embodiment of the productive scholar. He wrote voluminously in the fields of
history and of literature, and was perhaps at his best on problems where
the two regions coalesced, as they do in literary history. His research
was, however, independent; it was the product of his own interests,
pursued in the traditional way of culture and scholarship. It was not
part of a deliberate plan to establish a school of research wherein to train
others in the techniques of research. It did nevertheless initiate a process
which would eventually reach that stage. In fact, Ward's work led
straight to its consummation in Tout's achievement.

It was the Roscoe-Ward adoption of research as the directive and
formative factor in academic development which took Owens College
on its first big step forward towards university status. But, of course,
it was only with the passing of the years that the implications of the idea
were realised in practice and in import: and whilst the Roscoe-Ward
policy was gradually pervading the academic mind, other people were in
their own way making their contribution to the Manchester academic idea.
Before seeing the Roscoe-Ward impetus in closer detail it will be well to
see how others had prepared the way for them or had assisted in making
their projects possible. In the first place, the recognition of Roscoe and
Ward as pioneers in a new academic policy of research must not be
taken to mean that before Roscoe and Ward no one in Owens College
had realised the value of original thinking. Indeed, the first principal,
A. J. Scott, declared that the indispensable qualification of such teaching
staff as Owens College required was that all members of it should " dedicate themselves to the mastery and advancement of their several branches
of knowledge ", and this, he said, seemed " to be the definition of the
professor as distinguished from the minister of the earlier education ".
Scott's outlook, however, was fundamentally that of the moralist. His
conception of the pursuit of knowledge was that, as a mode of life, it
became for the student a " discipline in the solitary and abstract study "
which brings the scholar to his greatest good. " The congenial good of
the scholar lies in the truth, beauty and excellence of ideas; in plainer
words, it is enjoyed by knowing and contemplating." In effect, Scott's
outlook is entirely that of the teacher whose vocation is to endeavour
to lift his pupils to a higher plain of spiritual well-being by inducing in
them the habitual practice of an intellectual discipline. When he insists

E

that the prosecution of knowledge must be " completely unfettered by considerations of immediate application to use ", he is not, as sometimes in his confusing metaphysic he seems to imply, propounding a doctrine of the value of knowledge as, in itself, absolute for its own pure sake ; he is thinking not of the value of the thing known, but of the moral worth of the process of getting to know it.   It is his conviction that the incessant pursuit of learning is in itself a way perpetually to renew the life of the spirit.   It is the way to the scholar's good.   It is a mode of private life rather than a form of public service.   In the last resort, his final argument in support of the importance of the continuous searching after further knowledge is hardly a plea for research as such, or at least, for research as it tends to be conceived to-day.   It is rather a more general insistence on the indispensable worth of the explorative mind, and on the vitalising impulse of the spirit of enquiry.   As moralist and as teacher he realised that only by the inspiration of that spirit did a teacher teach effectively. Only those who themselves are continuously pushing forward through fresh fields of the mind can be real teachers of youth.   " The highest teaching can never be that of him whose chief business is to teach."   It is only the active scholar who can fulfil the real teacher's task.   " To catch information is something ; to catch the life and spirit of the pursuit and contemplation of truth is infinitely more."

Scott's major contribution to Owens College was his inculcation of a pervading sense of the dignity and the austerity of learning, of the value of knowledge as a part of eternal truth, and of the pursuit of it as a kind of secular service to achieve moral and religious ends.   It was, however, rather by the spirit of his teaching than by his technique in practising it that he exercised his influence.   His lectures were mainly for the elect ; for all the rest they were cloudy utterances beyond immediate comprehension.   They appeared hardly relevant to the nominal theme in the curriculum with which they were advertised to deal.   An occasional young listener was captured by the lure of metaphysical adventure.   But in Scott's time, few of the students were old enough in years or ripe enough in adequate schooling to get even a glimpse of the professor's trend of thought.   Owens' will made fourteen the minimum age of entry, and though the majority of the small band of early students consisted of somewhat older youths, these in general were without the background of a good systematic grounding in the elements of secondary education. Even the sons of relatively wealthy parents, whose schooling was paid for in private schools, as John Owens' had been, were regularly withdrawn to enter the family industry at fourteen or fifteen, as was John Owens himself.

Despite all this, however, Scott's doctrine of the dignity of knowledge was an invaluable basis on which to found the activities of Owens College. It is indeed the foundation stone of all university efforts. Besides this infiltration of a presiding academic atmosphere, Scott's service to the Owens College and Manchester University of the future is to be seen in his recognition of the need for popular adult education. He had been, and remained, a friend of F. D. Maurice ; he himself had lectured or preached in London on the Christian socialism which was Maurice's gospel at the time. Moreover, he knew of Maurice's foundation of the Working Men's College in London in 1854. At Manchester, he had very early (by 1852) instituted evening classes, but they were specifically designed for working schoolmasters whose days were spent in the schools. In 1858 his name appears, along with that of four of his professorial colleagues, on the management committee of the Working Man's College, which was brought into being in Manchester in 1858. But by then, Scott had resigned the Principalship of Owens, though he retained his chair until his death in 1866. He had never been happy in administrative work, and had shown no aptitude for it.

Scott's successor as principal was Greenwood, the professor of Latin and Greek. He was Principal from 1857 until 1889. When he entered on his new office, it looked as if Owens College was in danger of utter failure. The number of regular day-students had fallen by almost half —from 62 in 1851 to 34 in 1857. *The Manchester Examiner* described the college in that year as " going through its diurnal martyrdom of bootless enthusiasm and empty benches ". Greenwood, indeed, in the cautiousness of his nature and the lack of fire in his temperament, advocated turning the college into a school. However, very soon after becoming Principal of the College he began to direct the rebuilding of its academic foundation, and he watched over its progress right up to the attainment of its primary objective, the securing of university status. His greatest value to Owens was his unobtrusive mastery of the main arts of administration. In one of his few published lectures, he quoted an apt story of a man " who, conspicuous for the success and seeming ease with which he went through great labours, was asked for some hints of the system by which he accomplished so much. ' I have only one rule of action,' said he, 'that I know of.' 'What is that?' inquired the disciple, hoping that he was on the threshold of some great mystery. 'Why merely this, that whenever I have anything to do, I just do it.'" Greenwood just did in the quietest way what had to be done. What had to be done was, indeed, a huge job. Roscoe, looking back reminiscently in 1882 and recalling his own experiences—he had been in 1857 the first new appointment to the staff of Owens after Greenwood had been chosen as Principal —described those earlier years in these words: "To carry on manfully and hopefully the struggling of those early years, to dare to believe that Manchester was destined to become a seat of higher education, and that such an education would be eventually for, and welcomed by, our busy manufacturers and mercantile classes, to fight against half-hearted sympathy and even openly expressed contempt, these were the tasks which had to be undertaken and persevered in for years before any serious measure of success was achieved." Greenwood saw Owens College through this trying incubationary period. Without superlative distinction of mind, and without impressive force of character, he owed his success to his capacity for finding and getting on with the sort of people, more gifted in genius than himself, who would be the means of realising the Owens ideal. Himself a classical scholar, he had a generous appreciation of the worth of studies as remote from his own as were Roscoe's. He had a canny power of finding the right men as his professorial colleagues, the good sense afterwards to give them their heads, and a fair-minded and conciliatory disposition which made for successful co-operation in the common endeavour. His great service to Owens was the establishment and maintenance of a routine efficiency in the institution, by means of which it could move by progressive and cautiously calculated stages towards its academic objective. He contributed little to the Manchester idea itself. Scott had preached the dignity of learning as an austere ideal. Greenwood made the ideal more intelligible by translating it into the terms of a liberal culture, in the traditional sense which professors of Latin and Greek such as was Greenwood took that phrase to mean. When he became principal, the college had been branded as a " mortifying failure " by the liberal-minded *Manchester Guardian*: and in particular it had been blamed, not for doing inefficiently what it ought to be doing, but for doing efficiently what it ought not to be doing. It was, went the charge, misdirecting its energies in teaching the wrong things. The college was, so the *Manchester Guardian* said, dissipating itself in the propagation of a traditional classical curriculum. It was a charge the rebutting of which seemed particularly to fall on Greenwood. There is nothing strikingly original nor immediately impressive in his defence. His attitude of mind was to adopt those " principles of education " which have been " sanctioned by the wisdom and justified by the experience of past ages " : this he took to be the trust imposed by the founder when he ordained the teaching of " such branches of learning and science as are usually taught in the English Universities ". He maintained that the traditional subjects of education were taught primarily not for the value of the information they comprised, but for the sake of the intellectual discipline which they effected. Consequently he defended the " usefulness " of what was called a liberal education. In another of his published lectures he attacked what he conceived to be a false notion of the " impracticalness " of a liberal, as opposed to a professional, education. " In education, by some strange jugglery of language, *practical* is held to mean what has a tangible and sensible bearing (not on the business of life, this definition we should not object to, but) on a part of the business of life, and that part, one which educators have never professed to provide for, and education is declared unpractical if it does not almost exclusively aim at fitting the pupil for the details of a professional or mercantile career." The attack illustrates at once the orthodoxy, the traditionalism and the cautiousness of Greenwood. He was neither prophet nor reformer ; nor did he intuitively perceive the Manchester opportunity. But his temperament made him gradually responsive and then quickly amenable. His educational creed became, as he owned, that of Sir William Hamilton : " the highest end of education is not to dictate truths but to stimulate exertion ; since the mind is not invigorated, developed, in a word *educated*, by the mere possession of truths, but by the energy determined in their quest and contemplation ". Greenwood's standard, not only of curricula for students, but of the most important attribute to be sought in professional colleagues, was the measure of their " energy in the quest of truth ". Scott had placed the pursuit of truth as the function of universities ; Greenwood saw the kind of intellectual power by which the pursuit was best impelled. What, perhaps, he did not sufficiently realise was that the most potent energising force in the mind's pursuit of knowledge is that of imagination, the imagination which transforms the bare facts of knowledge of the past into the living substance of the present, and so gives to the disciple a zest for knowledge which is part of a zest for life itself.

Greenwood, however, was hardly the man to make his own subject, the classics, a new force in a new academic conception of culture. Indeed his orthodoxy led him to formulate the claim of the classical tradition in education much more absolutely than is consonant with to-day's opinion ; but he saw that in certain orbits of intellectual endeavour indispensable to the world of to-day, the classics were almost completely unhelpful. In the whole domain of the physical sciences, the modern world was immeasurably superior to the classical one. Recognising this as an historic fact, Greenwood was deliberately willing to do what intuitively he inclined to do, that is, to give Roscoe full scope to re-orientate the pattern of academic objectives. The prosecution of the physical sciences became the instrument by which the universities renewed their vitality by restoring their contact with the pressing needs of the world of their own day, and through which they explored ways and means which, whilst serving their particular purpose, also suggested modes of application to the pursuit of a truth even nearer to the ultimate than that which the physical universe alone can reveal. It was Greenwood's part as an administrator to provide the kind of machinery by which these new academic energies could flourish. And it was through his skill as administrator that he contributed most to the progress of the college ; he had little to add to the idea of the coming university, but he assisted in bringing his colleagues' ideas to practical realisation. Thus his day-to-day support of Roscoe, once Roscoe had converted him, smoothed the way to the future. In a larger and more public way, it was Greenwood's mastery of administrative detail and of administrative technique which put into their final form two signal pieces of legislation by which the college took two large strides towards university status. It was Greenwood who did most of the preparatory work for the Acts of Parliament by which in 1870 and 1871 Owens College became The Owens College with a widened scope of academic activity and larger and more unfettered resources by which to subsidise the wider scope. It was Greenwood also who through several years' negotiation arranged for the incorporation within the college of the Royal School of Medicine and of the provision of facilities at the Royal Infirmary for clinical teaching by the college's clinical professors. It is impossible to overestimate the importance of this amalgamation. As we have seen, even as early as 1836, there had been proposals, which nearly matured, to make the Royal Medical School the nucleus of a full-scale academic college. When Owens College came into existence, the Royal Medical School had been for a long time and was still a flourishing school of medicine : but until the college got on to its feet there was little point in seeking to incorporate a medical school. In the middle 'sixties, however, it became increasingly clear that the adequate provision of medical studies would not only enrich the collegiate work of the college, but it would lift it nearer to the level at which its claim for university status would be irrefutable. The college had already a professor, Williamson, who in the multiplicity of his nominal responsibilities for the natural sciences—he himself was primarily a botanist—was not only in charge of botany, zoology and geology, but had allotted to him such instruction as might be called for in " the anatomy and physiology of man as the highest type of animal organisation ". Williamson was also a qualified medical practitioner, and did in fact practise whilst he was a professor. Hence he was the member of Senate whose opinion would formally count as most pertinent in any question of the incorporation of a medical school within the function of the college. Yet it was he who led, or rather almost alone sustained, the opposition to any such incorporation. At this stretch of time since 1866, when Greenwood, probably at Roscoe's instigation, was eagerly pursuing means for the incorporation of the Royal Medical School with Owens, it is not easy to assess the validity of Williamson's professional arguments against the proposal ; they are mainly concerned with the conjectural reaction of medical teachers, medical practitioners and medical students to the proposed reorganisation. But at least one of his arguments has a curious interest. He held that the inclusion within the college of medical studies would be a menace to the moral welfare of the normal arts and science students ; for medical students, and especially medical students in the provinces—for the best went to London—were intellectually less sensitive and morally coarser than the average student, and so they would be a source of potential immorality. This argument must have been thought of some weight by the rest of the Senate who were in favour of the amalgamation, for they suggested that when medical students were admitted they might be segregated from all possibility of contact with Arts and Science students.

In effect the real gain of the amalgamation was seen at the outset by Roscoe, and has been demonstrated through every decade since the event. By the incorporation, Owens was strengthened by the addition of a new collegiate and academic discipline. It was moreover a discipline which, already conscious of its own reliance on the sciences of Physics and Chemistry, would participate in the normal academic pursuit of these subjects. Further still, by the union, the potential links between pure science and medicine were bound to become more patent ; medicine, too, would inevitably provide further stimulus to research, for new symptoms of disease are incessantly recurrent ; and, moreover, medicine would consciously or unconsciously be bound in the end to assert itself as the primary and most fundamental of the social sciences. It is an academic activity which is insistently reminded of its relation to the present, and an activity the pursuit of which must be immersed in the immediate and most clamorous needs of the people within its reach. The study of medicine is a magnificent safeguard against the pedantry which scorns the kind of education which is useful : and a useless education is a foolish contradiction of mere words. It can even be held that modern universities began with the Medical School at Salerno in the eleventh century. At all events, a medical curriculum is in some sense the pattern of the highest education, that is, it is a discipline in the art of utilising knowledge. More than any other of the faculties of a university it is the medical faculty which has best exemplified the way to that ideal attainment of a university, the discovery of the point at which learning and knowledge are active and activating moral and social ideas. No wonder that Ward and Roscoe found congenial minds in the medical professors who became part of Owens after the amalgamation. Indeed, in my own intercourse with academic colleagues in the last thirty-nine years, I would without hesitation say that it has been amongst my medical contemporaries that I have found not only the soundest academic conception of professional training, but also more frequently than in my own faculty a familiarity with the wider, traditional and non-professional content of what the world still acknowledges as the groundwork of a liberal culture. Moreover, if the rights of medicine as an integral part of an academic commonwealth have ever been questioned, surely the immediate response of academic faculties of medicine to play their part in the vastly increased services of medicine to the community provides a magnificent illustration of the real function of universities in our time : a capacity and a willingness to explore appropriate means for meeting the needs of a new social situation. So, when Greenwood stood for, and quietly secured, the union of the Royal Medical School and Owens College, he probably did his finest work for the Manchester University which was in due course to come into being.

In the same unobtrusive way, he made it his object to enlist to the

THE SENATE 1900

Reading from left to right. Standing : G. A. WRIGHT, W. H. PERKIN (*Junior*), H. L. WITHERS, R. B. WILD, F. A. SOUTHAM, A. JOHANNSON, W. A. COPINGER, J. DIXON MANN, E. FIDDES, A. W. FLUX, F. E. WEISS, W. J. SINCLAIR, S. J. HICKSON, J. DRESCHFELD, W. STIRLING. *Sitting :* S. ALEXANDER, T. H. CORE, H. B. DIXON, T. N. TOLLER, W. BOYD DAWKINS, O. REYNOLDS, A. HOPKINSON, A. S. WILKINS, A. SCHUSTER, J. S. SEATON, J. STRACHAN, A. H. YOUNG, H. LAMB, T. F. TOUT, V. KASTNER, A. S. DELÉPINE.

SOME OF THE FIFTY-ONE MEMBERS OF SENATE, 1944

Reading clockwise from Sir John Stopford, Vice-Chancellor, in the Chair : Sir John Stopford (*Vice-Chancellor*), W. J. Pugh (*Deputy Vice-Chancellor*), Donald Atkinson, L. E. Browne, A. H. Gibson, Edward Robertson, F. C. Wilkinson, Eugène Vinaver, H. B. Maitland, R. A. C. Oliver, R. A. Eastwood, L. J. Mordell, H. Graham Cannon, R. A. Cordingley, John Hollingworth, W. E. Morton, James Kenner, W. H. Semple, Sir James E. Myers (*Principal, College of Technology*), H. S. Raper, F. C. Thompson, E. F. Jacob, C. W. Wardlaw, F. P. Walton (*Assist. Registrar*), Norman Smith (*Registrar*).

staff of the college men who would follow in their own departments of enquiry developments parallel to those which Roscoe was prosecuting in science. Ward and Jevons came to chairs in 1866, and Osborne Reynolds in 1868. Jevons and Reynolds in their own fields welded the college more closely with the mind of Manchester, even as Roscoe was doing through his own particular science ; for economic thinking and engineering theory bore very directly on the questions which Manchester regarded as vital. But before the full impact of these newcomers could be felt, the college would have to escape from the stifling confinement and the increasing squalor of its home in Quay Street, although in the few intervening years before removal to fresh and more spacious quarters, Jevons may not have felt that the house in Quay Street which was the first Owens College and which had formerly been the residence of Richard Cobden, was an inappropriate place in which to develop economic doctrine. The immediate problem in the late 'sixties was the material one of rehousing on a new site ; and it was clear that the financial resources of the Owens Trust were insufficient to secure this. Greenwood, however, saw or was induced by Roscoe to see, that if means could be obtained to pay for a new site and new buildings, it might be possible by legal proceedings to empower the enlarged Owens to undertake academic activities not formally or nominally consonant with the terms of the original Owens Trust. With his customary administrative efficiency Greenwood set himself to achieve this. Roscoe was his main co-adjutator, and Roscoe captured the sympathy of Thomas Ashton, a great and characteristic leader of industrial and mercantile Manchester, whose participation in securing funds for the development of the present Oxford Road site was enough to make him the second, next to Owens the first, of our founders. Like Owens, he was the Manchester man incarnate : cotton manufacturer, Liberal, free-trader, philanthropically civic-minded. Unlike Owens he had had a university education at Heidelberg, and had a cultured interest in the fine arts as instruments of civilisation. He made the consolidation of Owens College his special form of social and civic service. The immediate result was a new home for the college on the Oxford Road site and a trebling of its financial endowment. To make full use of these additional resources, and to maintain the constitutional continuity of the original Owens College, powers were provided by two Acts of Parliament. The first, 1870, set up a new college, the Owens Extension College, and provided it with a public constitution which formed a new and more appropriate partnership of academic and civic authority in its government than was possible in a college like the original Owens College, which was governed by private trustees. The second Act of Parliament, 1871, amalgamated the original Owens with the new Extension College in a foundation to be called The Owens College, a college which would, at least to the extent of its new funds, be free, if it desired, to embark on forms of academic activity such, for instance, as the education of women, from which the letter of the Owens Trust debarred the original foundation. Once the new home and the new endowment were assured, the campaign for university status was begun in earnest. Greenwood, as principal, was its nominal leader. But the minds which gave substance and power to the shaping of the university which they were seeking to bring into being were mainly those of Roscoe and Ward. The intellectual strength of the college was gathering head in the 'sixties. As we have seen, Ward and Jevons came in 1866, and Osborne Reynolds became Manchester's first professor of Engineering in 1868.

The establishment of the chair of Engineering was brought about by the eager co-operation of most of Manchester's great engineering firms. Its institution is another landmark in our academic progress. For engineering is applied science : physics, mathematics and other sciences are its groundwork, but they must be applied to produce engines, and unless he can contribute to the production of engines, no man should be called an engineer. Engineering was the first indubitably " applied " science to be domiciled academically with the related sciences in the Manchester plan of studies. Its incorporation was a further demonstration of the validity of Roscoe's notion about the function of a university. The kind of vital contact between academic thought and local values which Roscoe from the first had sought to establish was visibly extending itself to other ranges of intellectual territory when Jevons expounded his economic doctrines and Reynolds turned his scientific investigations to the problems of the engineer. The bearing of Reynolds' work on the immediate and contingent welfare of Lancashire's heavy industry was plain to all. But in a much more subtle way, the mind of Jevons was admirably suited to infiltrate its quality of thought into the characteristic mentality of Manchester. It is not only that his theory of economics gave apparent validity to the commercial, industrial, and social habits of Manchester. It was also that his philosophic reconciliation of scientific discovery and religious belief was a doctrine very congenial to the Manchester men of the 'sixties and 'seventies. " I question whether any scientific works which have appeared since the *Principia* of Newton are comparable in importance to those of Darwin and Spencer, revolutionising as they do all our views of the origin of bodily, mental, moral and social phenomena." Nevertheless, accepting the conclusions of Darwin, Jevons does not believe that the progress of science will " result in dissipating the fondest beliefs of the human heart " ; indeed, a rigorous logical scrutiny will prove " the Reign of Law to be an unverified hypothesis, the uniformity of Nature an ambiguous expression, the certainty of scientific inference to a certain extent a delusion ". " Theologians have dreaded the establishment of the theories of Darwin and Spencer as if they thought that those theories could explain everything upon the purest mechanical and material principles, and exclude all notions of design ; they do not see that those theories have opened up more questions than they have closed ; we cannot disprove the possibility of divine interference."

Roscoe, as was seen, had started the direct path to the sort of university which Owens was to become : and when Ward came to be his partner in building up the academic policy for Manchester, a comprehensive and well-balanced development was assured. What jointly and complementarily they stood for will more clearly appear if they are first looked at separately. Roscoe's advocacy of research as the vitalising spirit of academic corporations had already been noted. But besides that item of belief, he had strong views on other aspects of academic habit and aim. Roscoe believed that education ought not to be purely literary and that literary scholarship was too exclusively regarded as the only way to the attainment of what was called culture. The study of the (physical) sciences, he held, involved a perpetual exercise of intellectual enquiry, whereas in their earliest stages literary studies consisted largely in the accumulation of information by memory. Roscoe's first task in Manchester was to convince the public that Science could be made an efficient instrument of education and that such an education was not only compatible with, but absolutely necessary for, a successful manufacturing and industrial career. He records in his memoirs that it was a far from easy task to convince the Trustees of the college that a mere repetition on an insignificant scale of the old university idea of a mainly classical training could not be expected to succeed in Manchester ; nor was it easy to bring home to them that unless the new institution was to sink down to the level of a school (as many in the despairing mood of apparent failure were advocating in 1857) or to die out altogether, some new line had of necessity to be pursued. He urged them to see the opportunity for this in the study of physical science. Perhaps retrospectively—and the remarks quoted above were written in 1887—Roscoe exaggerated the difficulties with the Trustees ; for, as we have seen, the committee of Trustees made specific preparation for Chemistry in their original plan. His suggestion, too, that the stipend attached to his chair indicated the Trustees' opinion of its relative unimportance as a subject is not quite just : it was paid less because it would not require the full-time services of the professor. The Trustees, in fact, seem to have given him cordial support in his enterprise. The dominant motive in his public application of his professorial life was to cure English industry of its greatest weakness, " its singular want of appreciation of one of the essential conditions of success, viz., a sound and thorough training in the scientific principles which underlie all practice ". He felt that our national economy was at stake. " Unless we set up a more profound and intimate connection between Science and Practice, our continental rivals who practise with knowledge must in the long run out-bid our own manufacturers who practise by rule of thumb." From his point of view, he had to build up a belief in the efficacy of scientific training. He had to prove to the practical man that " youths trained in the Chemistry School at Owens College were able not only to take a more intelligent part in the operations of the various manufactures than those who had not had such advantages, but that this education had given an insight into these processes such that those thus trained were able to effect improvements or even to make discoveries of importance." Very quickly Roscoe won success. Owens College soon became the only English college in which chemical training and chemical investigation were being carried on by similar methods and in a similar spirit to those which Roscoe had learnt under Bunsen at Heidelberg.

The earlier planners of Owens College had found the Scottish universities the most helpful models from which to get ideas for their own institution. Later, Roscoe saw how much could be learnt from the universities of Germany. It was not only by taking over their scientific methods and thus domiciling research within the academic structure that Roscoe brought from Germany a new academic principle. His practice of the principle led directly or indirectly to the opening up of new sources from which Manchester University was to draw immense strength. From about the middle of the century onwards, political events on the Continent were causing many men of business and commerce, more especially Germans, to seek a permanent home in England, and particularly in and about Manchester. Many who were concerned with engineering, with the cotton industry, and with merchanting settled in Manchester and built up highly successful commercial and industrial organisations. They were attracted by Roscoe's academic ideas; and their interest was increased when Roscoe brought Schorlemmer from Germany in 1874 to fill in Manchester the first British chair of Organic Chemistry. A good number of these new citizens of Manchester did what they could to co-operate with the college; and down the years many of them have acted in the full and formal sense as members of our governing body. In a more material way, as a glance at the list of our benefactors will show, they have from time to time made very considerable contributions to our financial resources. But beyond that, they have been, as if instinctively, sympathetic supporters of the social and cultural ideas for which the college and then the University has stood. They were intellectually like-minded with the broadly liberal social outlook of the University. Even more, they displayed amongst us a range of interests and of æsthetic sensitiveness which hitherto had been much more a casual than a regular item in the life of our successful men of commerce and industry. On the Continent, music and the pictorial arts were traditionally a part of the culture, and of the leisured occupations, of the bourgeois industrial and commercial leaders. Through their influence, a German, Charles Hallé, settled in Manchester, and put it on to the cultural map of Europe; and in many ways, they played their part in the encouragement of sculpture and painting. In this manner, they were bringing to the Manchester climate of opinion a stream of spiritual values which gradually incorporated themselves with the already established moral culture of the native Mancunian, and so provided an intellectual atmosphere invaluable to the progress of the academic idea.

Apart from this wider consequence of Roscoe's linking of Manchester with Germany's civic and academic culture, his institution in his own department of the specifically German approach to his own range of scientific interests meant not only that the notion of higher education was the richer for the inclusion in it of a new kind of discipline, but that learning and research were identified in a new conception of scholarship. It not only meant these things in the fundamental and central principle of academic life. It also meant that in its strictly academic energies the college was linking itself more closely with the interests of its region. Roscoe was civic and social minded. He was a keen politician ; in later life he became a Liberal Member of Parliament. It seemed to him sheer stupidity to deprive women of higher academic education. He was also deeply interested in popular adult education. Not only did he conduct, as all the early professors of Owens conducted, regular evening classes, but in 1862, during the period of extensive unemployment in the cotton industry, he organised popular lectures on a wide range of subjects as some kind of relief for the out-of-works. The lectures were so successful that four years later he started a series of Popular Penny Science Lectures for Working People. He invited very distinguished scientists, including Huxley, Tyndale, and Avebury, to give a lecture or several lectures in some large hall or other in a poor part of Manchester. The lecture was printed forthwith, and copies sold at one penny each. The success of the course in the first year led to more ambitious plans. Besides lectures, classes in elementary chemistry were organised : and the fame of the lectures grew so much that a hall as big as the Free Trade Hall would on occasion be packed with listeners.

It is less easy to specify the distinctive contribution of Ward to the evolving Manchester idea. He had a high sense of the importance of university training, university life, and university influence. When he was appointed to Manchester in 1866, he was one of the few of its professors who had full experience of life in our ancient universities : he had been an undergraduate at Peterhouse College, Cambridge. He attached a high value to the collegiate aspects of university life even in a non-residential university. In an academic community, men are joined in fellowship and freedom to a common high purpose, and the functions of learning to work and learning to live are not separate : " the one comprehends the other, we serve our generation, our country and the better future of a better world by what our lives and this training have made us, of which our knowledge, our skill, our very aspirations are only part ". Collegiate life is, he held, a system of intellectual intercommunion between fellow-students, between teachers and learners, united together by a consciousness of belonging to the same community. A university is in essence of a double nature, it is a place of education and a place of learning, holding a right balance between the effort devoted to the distribution of existing knowledge and that given to the acquisition of new. The work of instruction in it must not unduly overshadow the pursuit of learning and scientific research. Its persisting manner must be the communication to the minds of youth not only of science which is in a state of completeness, but also of science which is in a state of growth ; in that way the student is brought into contact with the living elements that make up the progress of human culture.

It will be obvious that Ward the arts man rested primarily on more traditional intellectual foundations than did Roscoe. By a political analogy, Roscoe might be thought of in academic outlook as a Radical, and Ward as a Whig. Indeed, Ward's own addiction to the scholarly life was the nineteenth-century version of Gibbon's eighteenth-century practice of learning. Scholarship in itself was a way of civilised life, a gentleman's contribution to the understanding of a past on which modern civilised society had perforce to build itself. Ward was the *privat Gelehrte* ; his research was the continuous product of his unintermittent intellectual hobby. But by his writings, he was exemplifying a process in which some of the methods of scientific research could, by appropriate adaptation, serve the purposes of humanist and especially of historical scholarship. Doing so, he was illustrating how humanistic research could transcend its congenital danger, the danger of being concerned with merely verbal entities, and of thus being a mere instrument for the propagation and transmission of inert ideas. Ward's own lines of research were in no sense romantically venturesome. They were conventionally determined enquiries, which did not seek to break into strange regions of the unknown. He set himself to retell the tale of the past in the light of fuller information and in order to make its course and its significance more intelligible to the present. It was indeed real " research ". But it was not the sort of research which, whilst calling for its prosecutor's imaginative insight into human motive, at the same time stimulated the imaginative participation of those to whom it was recounted. Ward the researcher never gave to Ward the teacher that imaginative spell which vitalises the transmission of factual knowledge. His lectures, like his books, were dignified and impressive ; but impressive rather than inspiring. Hence, he did not contribute greatly in his own range of scholarship to the solution of the major problem of university life, namely, the coalescence in identity of the two main activities of a university, its function to educate and its function to research. But by being himself a researcher Ward was at least making the problem clear. Moreover, he was continually agitating for undergraduate schools in which the rudiments of research methods could be inculcated, and for the corporate undertaking of planned research by trained researchers. But in Manchester, circumstance limited him rather to devising than implementing a school of research. He had, however, set the situation, and he had profoundly influenced his junior colleague, Tout, who, in due course widely developed the Ward plan and brought it to fruition.

To the more general problems of academic development Ward brought a wide political wisdom. He insisted that in an academic community the co-ordination of all the studies which it comprised should be effected by co-operation, and without assumption of a preferential place for one or the other. A true university idea incorporates all the great branches of studies ; a Faculty of Arts is strengthened by a Faculty of Science, and the balance between them seems likely to maintain itself as if by a law of nature. The incorporation of the physical sciences into an academic community had proved to be a widening and a deepening of the essential idea of a university. Hence Ward was wholeheartedly in sympathy with Roscoe and with Roscoe's notion of academic science. In the obituary notice which Ward wrote of Roscoe many years later (1915), he noted particularly that Roscoe was " one of those who at an early date perceived the futility of any attempt to separate ' technical ' from other branches of secondary and higher education, and who recognised the imperative need, in the best interests of the country, of a constant inter-penetration of practical and theoretical disciplines ". Indeed in every direction Ward sought to strengthen the intellectual links between the University and its region. Opening the session in 1894, he said that the University was not an Artemisium in the midst of Ephesus or any such-like separation of town and gown ; on the contrary by the very conditions of its origin and existence, it was a monument of civic effort, and in the purport of its occupations a part of civic life. Twenty years earlier, when the Manchester Medical School was incorporated with Owens College, he had eagerly welcomed the event, and, in 1894, looking backwards he regarded it as one of the happiest pages in the college history : the pleasure and stimulus of daily intercourse with fellow-workers in Medicine, in Science, and in Arts had been a great enrichment to the college both as a place of education and a place of research. The more a university opened its doors to all branches of study the more it was adding to its vigour in the corporate pursuit of its highest endeavour as a university.

No one more than Ward strengthened in the University this characteristic conception of the union and unity of all branches of knowledge, as well as of the academic dedication of them to high ideals. Adamson, who was professor of Philosophy in Manchester from 1876 to 1893, and therefore a colleague of Ward's during all those years, translated the Ward view into even wider terms. In an article in the *Owens College Magazine* (1878) he protested against the notion that the literary disciplines were more humane and more catholic in interest than the sciences; he denied that literary studies were the sole true representatives of culture. It was impossible, he said, to claim for any of the branches of literature a deeper, more intimate connection with the ultimate questions of human interest than is held by general Biology or general Physics. A Faculty of Science, he said, need never fear to assert its rights so far as culture is concerned. This was a point of view which Adamson shared with Ward. It helps to explain Ward's success as the principal of a college like Owens, for in some superficial and personal ways, he hardly seemed the ideal man for such a post. What Ward really was, and what he did, has been admirably summarised by Tout in a foreword he wrote to a Bibliography of Ward which was published by the Cambridge University Press in 1926. " As a scholar he won distinction in widely different literary and historical fields. As a teacher and writer he was a stimulus to many generations of disciples, some now grown old, who have achieved fame in very different walks of life. He was a leader in the vindication of the right of history and modern literature to obtain academic recognition, and of the claim of women to share fully in the opportunities of men to obtain higher education. As an academic administrator he was foremost among the makers of a new university, and the reformers of an old one. But, great as was his achievement, it counts for little as compared with the personality and character which inspired it. Critics might complain that his scholarship with all its width was seldom ultimate, that his academic leadership was sometimes tempered by prudent opportunism, and that his devotion to detail sometimes obscured the basic principles which inspired him. But there could only be one opinion of the man. His very presence was an inspiration and made him an ideal leader. Tall, dignified, gravely magnificent in manner, he bore, in middle life, a striking physical resemblance to his cousin, Matthew Arnold, though few men were more unlike in their general attitude of mind. He was sometimes said to have inherited the manners of the diplomatist of the older school, courteous and urbane

F

but somewhat formal, aloof, and haughty. But this was a very superficial view of one of the most kindly, friendly, and sympathetic of men. His stately manner could obscure, only to very unseeing eyes, the warmth of his affections and the kindliness and simplicity of his nature."

What may well be called the Roscoe-Ward version of the idea of Owens College as a university was sharply crystallised by circumstance in the 1870's. As has been seen, by the acts of 1870 and 1871, a new academic government had been set up. Moreover, a new site had been found, new activities had arisen from the incorporation of the Medical School, and through the energies and driving force of Thomas Ashton new endowments were being built up. Within the college, scholarship was being strengthened by the recruitment of new professors, and by an acceleration of the process by which the hitherto ludicrously wide fields of learning for which professors were individually responsible were more specifically limited. Principal Scott, for instance, besides being Principal, was in 1857 professor of English Language and Literature, of Comparative Grammar, of Hebrew, of Logic, and of Mental and Moral Philosophy. R. C. Christie was in 1854 professor of History, and in 1855 he took on also the professorship of Political Economy and that of Jurisprudence and Law. Ward himself was in 1866 appointed professor of English Language and Literature and also of History. The newcomers to chairs in the 1870's included, besides Adamson, Wilkins, Hopkinson, Schorlemmer and Boyd Dawkins: and also, of course, professors in the new Medical School, such as Dreschfeld and Morgan: like Schorlemmer, Dreschfeld brought to Manchester the academic German attitude to science, and he established it where it was invaluable, namely in the Manchester Medical School, of which he had been a student, and in which he was now to be a powerful scientific influence.

Under such auspices the official campaign to secure university status was launched. There was a spear-head committee of four, Greenwood, Roscoe, Ward and Morgan, who drafted and circulated a series of documents and memoranda. In doing this, they had perforce to formulate their notions about what sort of a university Owens College wished to become. They put the case first to the public through the press. They also took advice from distinguished academic people; and they circulated replies received from these persons, as well as articles occasioned in the public press. Finally they framed their request in an official Memorial to the Crown.

They claimed that the spread of secondary education was producing a large number of promising students, drawn from classes now for the first time finding education at their disposal, but finding also that there was not available for them education at the higher post-school level. What little there was was too expensive (one remembers the plea of the Petitioners for a Manchester University in 1640), and was also in many ways unsuitable because of its lack of provision for modern and for scientific studies. Universities appropriate for such a clientèle were an urgent national need. They should, like the Scottish universities, and still more, like continental ones, be set in the heart of great centres of industry and commerce. In support of these views, the committee printed considerable and varied testimony. Sir Benjamin Brodie, professor of Chemistry in the University of Oxford, supported Manchester strongly, asserting that Oxford was no place for a student of moderate means and of industrious and frugal habits ; it was far more expensive than it need be, and the cost arose not so much from the expense of the education itself as from the habits of the place : moreover, Oxford's attempt to develop the pursuit of the sciences had to struggle against the traditions and the prestige of an essentially medieval system of studies. Professor Jack, who had just left the chair of Natural Philosophy at Owens on succeeding to a professorship in Glasgow, urged that Owens had in fact already earned university status. It had as many students as had Aberdeen. It had a body of eminent professors, and it had grown in its own rights and by its own momentum ; and in that respect it was vitally different from what he referred to as the pathetic University of Durham, " founded on the initiative of the Government and of a corporation which had too much money, founded ' in the air ', and settled upon ' a consideration ' ". The great argument in Manchester's favour, Jack went on, was " its intimate relations with the wants of the district " ; its professors were thus enabled to give their higher teaching an appropriate organisation. The most pointed letter of support for the Owens' idea was from the Right Honourable Dr. Lyon Playfair, M.P., F.R.S., who had been professor of Chemistry in the Manchester Institute in the 1840's. This is a quotation from it. " I have always thought that Owens College ought to develop into a ' teaching University '. England contains no teaching University like the Scotch and German Universities. They have kept to the original purpose of most Universities, *viz.* to liberalise the education of professions and the occupations of life. Oxford and

Cambridge (on the other hand) have exalted the preparatory pedagogium, or Arts Faculty, to be the end instead of the beginning of the Universities, and thus have cut themselves off from the professions. They are worthy universities of a class, that is, of men of wealth and leisure . . . but they are not Universities of the nation. Durham has lately, through Newcastle, been trying to get back to the original intention of Universities, but she is too ecclesiastical to succeed. Manchester can become a teaching University for England with the specific object of liberalising professions and industrial occupations. . . . If you keep clearly in view the essential difference between Oxford and Cambridge and the truly national Universities, you may make out a strong case." So, in 1876, Playfair posed the Oxbridge-Redbrick problem, and, perhaps, more pertinently than more recent academic theorists.

Owens College claimed that it " had already attained to a life and character of its own ". It had consistently followed its original charge. " The primary or immediate work of Owens College is to supply Manchester and its district with genuine academical culture for its future merchants and manufacturers and for others who by reason of good parts and aspiring natures may seek such culture : it likewise has to maintain and develop its character as a place of research and learning, where teachers and students shall in conjunction pursue the several branches of academical study with a view to their continuous advance in the world of science and letters." Owens College could therefore claim that it " had arrived at a stage in its history when it depends upon the actual character of its teaching, upon the spirit that its teaching is able to infuse into its students, and upon the work those students will in consequence accomplish in and beyond their college course, whether its progress is to be merely one in numbers and outward proportions, or one corresponding to Professor Huxley's conception of a live University ". Of course, the idea of Owens was to become a University fulfilling the functions prescribed by Huxley : " A University is, in my judgment, a corporation which has charge of the interests of knowledge as such, and the business of which is to represent knowledge by the acquirements of its members, to increase knowledge by their investigations, to diffuse knowledge by their teaching ; and last, but not least, to create a respect for knowledge among their fellow men by their personal example and influence." This was exactly the notion of the Manchester University-to-be as it was conceived by Roscoe and Ward. Huxley, too, believed it desirable that such a body

THE QUADRANGLE, *circa* 1890

THE OXFORD ROAD FRONTAGE, *circa* 1926
(*From an etching*)

THE OXFORD ROAD FRONTAGE WITH THE WHITWORTH HALL, 1902

as he described should exist in every great centre of population so that its advantages could be accessible to every member of the population.

In particular, Owens urged that its location and its local function gave it positive advantages as a potential university. " University teaching is in this as in other countries extending not only in the range of *subjects*, in some of which, such as the various branches of physical science, of engineering and mechanics, and of medicine, the older seats of learning have little or no advantage over more modern schools, or are placed in a positively disadvantageous relation towards them. Thus, in the case of medical training, Oxford and Cambridge cannot supply the invaluable adjunct of large hospitals near at hand. Academical instruction is also—and more especially in England where it has so long been in general confined to particular classes of society—endeavouring to meet the demands of a far wider range of *students*, who are desirous of entering upon higher and fuller courses of study, but who at the same time are practically unable to resort to Oxford or Cambridge. A new *stratum* of society, and a constantly increasing one, has been opened to the influences of University life, and it is absolutely necessary for the progress of the country at large, and for the greatness and security of its future, that means should be found for meeting the growing demand in question." It was, they urged, especially in science that a desire for higher training had made itself manifest in the Manchester district : it was in Manchester, too, that the teaching of science, through the labours of Dalton before the existence of Owens College, and later of Joule, had been associated with original scientific investigation. A Manchester University would inevitably regard itself as in duty bound to prosecute research in all departments of knowledge. The College, it was claimed, had now a large and growing number of students who were following regular and planned courses of study for three or four years. Even the bulk of the evening students did so. Moreover, though fourteen was the nominal age of permitted entry, an insignificant number came before they were sixteen, and practically half the total number of students were over eighteen. There was then ample material through which to conduct a great experiment in university education. But a prerequisite condition for the experiment was a charter conferring the right to award degrees. Though Huxley had strongly supported the recognition of Owens College as a place of university education in the highest sense, he had doubted the wisdom of giving it the right (in his own phrase), " to brand its own herrings ".   But, on the spot, Manchester knew far better.   Its professors must model their courses and their classes to their own problems : otherwise, there could be no real experiment and no academic discovery.   In support of this fundamental need, Owens College published an extract from a speech by Mark Pattison given in 1876, and well worth reprinting here as an assessment of the achievements of Owens College by an independent observer whose life had been lived in the conventional academic world of Oxford.   It was an address on Education given before the Social Science Congress on 13th October, 1876.

"I have spoken only of our old Universities, or rather of Oxford, because I know it best.   But I must not forget that there are younger institutions which are struggling upwards towards the ideal of a University, as I have described it in Professor Huxley's words—' a corporation which has charge of the interests of knowledge as such '.   At the head of these I must place Owens College—not only because it is in Lancashire, but because in its staff of professors it possesses a body of men who are truly representative of knowledge in a variety of its most important departments. In a single generation we have seen this College rise from humble beginnings to a position in which it can put forward a claim to be incorporated as a University, with the privilege of giving degrees.   Its capitalised sources are, indeed, small.   In addition to the original £100,000 of Owens's bequest, about £220,000 has been contributed by voluntary subscribers, an insignificant sum when compared with the wealth of the great manufacturing metropolis.   These funds, too, have been raised almost exclusively in a very small circle and by a very few public-spirited individuals ; they have not been drawn from the general mass of manufacturing wealth in Manchester or the neighbouring district.   With material means so inadequate, the scientific eminence attained by this young institution is a remarkable example of intellectual vigour which must dispose us to regard favourably its claims to incorporation.   But there is, besides, an immediate practical requirement which compels Owens College to seek without delay the right of conferring degrees. It is this, that as long as its students are under the necessity of graduating through the University of London they must pass through the examinations required for the London degree, consequently the professors of Owens College can never take the free and independent position of teachers of science.   It is inevitable that they must prepare their pupils for examination, and every true teacher knows too well that this process is incompatible with genuine instruction in letters and science. The efficiency of a local University is not to be measured by the amount of its annual income, nor its success by the number of its pupils. Does it profess to teach and represent human knowledge in all its main branches and in its most complete forms ? Is each great department occupied by men who are in possession of the long traditions of the past and zealous in searching out what still remains unexplored ? Is liberal culture recognised as its basis, and progressive science as its aim ? Where these conditions are fulfilled it would be hard to say why such an institution should not be entrusted by the State with the privilege of marking its students with the public stamp of certified acquirement. If it were merely a question of comparative qualification it would be difficult to maintain that Durham possesses and that Owens College does not possess the capacities, extensive and intensive, which I have supposed to be required. But if in the next twenty years the growth of Owens College is in proportion to its advance in the last twenty, the question will by that time have settled itself ". So said Mark Pattison in 1876.

The campaign succeeded up to a point. Owens College received university status in 1880, but it was not quite in the form which had been sought. Meeting difficulties in securing absolute independence, it had accepted a compromise in which it became the first college in a federal university, the Victoria University, with its seat in Manchester. But at least it had secured large freedom. Its professors, together with those of other colleges which might be admitted into the federation, would design their own curricula and their own examinations. To that extent 1880 makes the Roscoe-Ward idea of a Manchester University a legal reality.

CHAPTER V
FEDERAL TO FREE UNIVERSITY: THE SCHUSTER-TOUT EPOCH

THE work of the next twenty years was to use the new freedom to explore the hitherto untried and, in some cases, the unsuspected resources and capacities of the organism which the Owens' idea had generated. Still, and rightly, the major concern was to strengthen and enlarge its provision of learning and scholarship, but for scholarship which by now was almost automatically regarded as the liberal and catholic pursuit of all kinds of learning and science. Between 1880 and 1890 Schuster, Stirling, Lamb and Dixon were appointed to chairs. In 1890, Ward succeeded Greenwood as Principal, holding the office until 1898 when Alfred Hopkinson succeeded him. Between 1890 and 1904, Tout, Alexander, Perkin, Hickson, Weiss and Peake became professors in Manchester. Hence, by the middle 'nineties the large progress made in extending the University's functions began to make the federal system more and more inadequate to growth, experiment, and adaptation.

Agitation was begun to secure complete independence, and in 1903 Owens College was released from all federal obligation and became the independent Victoria University of Manchester in 1904.

In the meantime, in 1901, the college reached its jubilee although, for good reasons, the official celebration was deferred until the following year. The public recognition of the extent to which in its growth it had followed exploratively along the lines of its first idea was best expressed on that occasion in an address from " The University of Paris, the oldest of the Universities " :

Paris

Au Collège Owens de L'Université Victoria

L'Université de Paris

MY LORD

MESSIEURS ET TRÈS HONORÉS COLLÈGUES,

L'Université de Paris, la plus vieille des Universités, apporte à votre

Collège, qui est une des plus jeunes écoles de haute culture ses félicitations pour l'œuvre accomplie par lui en un demi-siècle, et ses vœux pour l'avenir.

Le Collège Owens a le rare mérite de remplir tous les devoirs et fonctions de l'enseignement supérieur : garder l'antique patrimoine des humanités, qui, étant commun aux peuples civilisés, est pour eux comme un rappel à la fraternité ; travailler au progrès de la science, pour l'honneur de l'intelligence humaine et pour ajouter aux victoires de l'esprit sur la matière : collaborer à l'œuvre démocratique de l'éducation populaire. En effet, vous donnez leur part aux humanités, puisque vous formez des lettrés et des artistes ; vous instruisez des ingénieurs, ces officiers de la guerre pacifique ; et, par vos cours du soir, par l'extension universitaire, vous élevez le niveau intellectuel de vos artisans.

À ces obligations diverses, les vieilles universités s'efforcent de satisfaire, en se transformant. Votre Collège s'est trouvé tout d'abord adapté aux besoins des temps nouveaux. Il a eu l'heureuse fortune de naître dans une des capitales de l'industrie moderne, et de s'incorporer si bien en elle que les deux destinées semblent confondues : le Collège Owens est une grande maison intellectuelle, que seule la reine du coton pouvait, en cinquante années, porter au point où nous la voyons aujourd'hui.

My lord,

Messieurs et très honorés collègues,

Tout le monde doit vous être reconnaissant d'avoir prouvé, par votre memorable exemple, que les temps sont passés où l'on pouvait scinder en deux parts le champ de l'activité humaine, n'honorer que la manifestation de la pensée speculative ou esthétique et rejeter à un rang infime les travaux qui étendent chaque jour l'empire de l'homme sur la nature.

Laissez-nous ajouter que nous ne saurions oublier, en cette circonstance solennelle, ni les glorieux échanges qui se sont faits au cours des siècles entre les philosophes et penseurs de l'Angleterre et ceux de la France, ni la grande gloire de Manchester, reconnue par tous ceux qui étudient l'histoire de la liberté dans le monde moderne. Liberté politique, liberté économique, liberté religieuse, toutes les libertés, Manchester les a reclamées et fait triompher à leur heure. L'Université de Paris se plaît à rendre hommage à ce souvenir.

Paris, en Sorbonne, le 5 Mars 1902.

Le Vice-Recteur, Président du Conseil de l'Université,

GREARD.

Le Secrétaire du Conseil,

E. LAVISSE.

The diagnosis, in this tribute, to the distinctive contribution of Manchester's Owens College in the progress of university history is remarkably apt. The naming of its part in preserving the humanities and developing them as elements binding civilisation together in a common culture ; in pursuing science as both an education and a conquest of nature by man ; and in acting as a direct social force for the raising of the general level of thought amongst the people—all these are implicit in the original idea of the ordinary Manchester merchant whose name was John Owens. Even more remarkable is the naming of Owens College as the outstanding example of a great triumph, the reconciliation of the sciences and the arts as essential and interrelated elements in any real conception of academic culture, the recognition, in fact, of what Roscoe and Ward had achieved in a re-orientation of academic philosophy. Lastly there is the Vice-Recteur's recognition that the underlying spirit of Owens was a sense of the infinite value of freedom of thought, and, with it, freedom from subscription to religious tests. This was the freedom John Owens conferred on Owens College, the freedom recalled to the students by Sir Benjamin Brodie in a speech at the opening of the new home of Owens College in 1873 : " I earnestly hope and steadily believe that Owens College will ever preserve that union between freedom and science, freedom not only to think, but freedom of research and freedom of speech, which is absolutely necessary for the progress of science ; I hope that nobody will ever meddle with your professors and try to put an extinguisher upon their researches."

One other item from the proceedings at the celebration of the Jubilee is worth recalling. The Prince of Wales was present to open the Whitworth Hall on Wednesday, 12th March, 1902. On behalf of the college, Sir Frank Forbes Adam, later to be chairman of the Council of the University, expressed the college's gratitude to the Prince and Princess. In the course of his speech, he put into one paragraph a summary account of what Owens was intended to be, what it had been, and what it would continue to be, the persisting and formative idea of the place, recognised and characterised as a common article of Manchester faith. " Building on sure foundations laid by our predecessors, following on the lines marked out by them, inspired by their example, we may confidently look forward to still further expansion and progress till we attain to that perfected, complete and all-embracing ideal that will enable us to offer to the most capable youth of Manchester and surrounding towns and districts, of neighbouring counties, and perhaps from a wider and more distant circle, the opportunity of obtaining a final and crowning intellectual training and equipment, a training that will qualify them to fulfil in every department of life's activities their duty to themselves, their county and the United Kingdom, and to contribute to the strength and permanent supremacy of that Empire which is the wonder and, alas, the envy of the world."

Just as the Roscoe-Ward partnership had marked one definitive stage in the further realisation of the Owens idea, the next stage may be said to have been effected by the partnership of Schuster and Tout in the 1890's and the following decade. As, however, the pattern of the future was already becoming more and more obvious, and as the day to day activities of the University were increasing enormously in bulk and in reach, it comes more and more invidious to try to distinguish between the many who in their own ways were exercising a vital influence on the progress of the University. Moreover, much of the value of their influence lay in the vigour which they devoted to the many-sided nature of their duties, to teaching, to administration, to scholarship, as well as in another direction, to what Sadler called the University's " pastoral " work in its province, its extra-mural activities of all kinds. They never for a moment regarded the University as an ivory tower in an academic pleasaunce. As, however, our particular interest is to watch in the expansion of the Owens idea the ways by which its distinctive function became more and more conscious, and thus opened up more and more directions for organic growth, only those of the many fellow-workers in the process who were given to frequent or comprehensive exposition of their own notion of what the University was or should be will provide the material appropriate to this section of our argument. By the nature of it, preference must be given to those who were more continuously or more passionately interested in declaring their conception of our academic

function. In any event, from 1890 to 1925, the years during which Tout
was a Manchester professor, what seem to have been the most powerful
trends of distinctive opinion in shaping and defining our policy are those
which were promulgated by Schuster, by Tout, and by Alexander. Of
course, in and throughout the meantime, scientists and scholars in the
University were pursuing their scientific and scholarly work : for instance,
a man like Rutherford was adding incalculable authority to Manchester
as an academic centre by his own contributions to the supreme academic
activity of universities, their extension of the boundaries of knowledge.
But even Rutherford, and with him a score of others whose names endure
in the history of science and scholarship, will perforce find no more than
a mention in this volume.

Schuster was academically a disciple of Roscoe ; he shared Roscoe's
view of the part to be played by the natural sciences in a university.
Like Roscoe he was especially interested in the bringing of science and
industry together, and in the problem immediately rising from this,
namely, the extent to which industrial applications of science should take
their place in a university curriculum. He specifically addressed himself
to the " connection between pure and applied science ". He pointed out
that practical experiment had historically preceded the formulation of
theoretic science. Even mathematics, " the purest of all sciences ",
arose from practical requirements. The very name, geometry, for one
of the more abstract branches of mathematics, indicates its origin in
practical expedients for measuring land. Algebra, even more abstract,
took over at its starting-point plus and minus signs from the weights-
notation of commercial warehouses.

Archimedes was led to discover the laws of hydrostatics because he
wanted an answer to a practical problem, an estimate of the amount of
gold and of alloy in a particular king's particular crown. Leonardo da
Vinci, in his turn, was first of all the practical man. " In investigating
problems of nature ", wrote da Vinci, " I first perform a few experiments,
because it is my plan to put the question in terms of actual experience,
and then try to show why things which happen in nature do happen in
that way." " Mechanics is the paradise of mathematical science, for
through mechanics we obtain the fruits of mathematics." The experimental method has been historically the way to the extension of science.
Schuster added as his own opinion about the progress of science this
summary conclusion on what one could learn from history of the relative

F. E. WEISS, Vice-Chancellor 1913–1915

value of the theoretic and the experimental scientist. " There have of course at all times been men of a speculative turn of mind who endeavoured to derive metaphysical systems from supposed facts and laws of nature. However interesting the writings of such men are to us now, however important they are in other respects, they had very little influence, and certainly no beneficial influence, on the progress of science. Through the cumulative evidence of experimentalists, modern scientific theory was really founded by Galileo and Newton. But practical application was the impulse which first inspired scientists ; and practical application will still be a primary force in prompting the further development of science. The teaching of the industrial applications of science cannot be separated from the teaching of science itself." That is Schuster's considered policy. How will such introduction affect the proper functions of a university ? Will it be for good or for evil ? To him the problem was a realistic one. A determining factor was this : social and economic forces had radically altered the relationship of academic people to the community. " The barriers are broken down which divided the man who spent his life in quiet study from the one who gave himself up to commercial and industrial pursuits ", and " no one will regret that university training is brought within the reach of the commercial classes ". For that part of a university's function which is to provide a discipline for the exercise of the human faculties, it can no longer be maintained that " a sound training either in mathematics or in classics is a sufficient preparation for whatever line a student might follow in after life ". Hence the University must admit a much wider range in its span of academic subjects, and, in the first instance, the extension must be for the inclusion of those branches of knowledge which spring from the struggles of real life as it is lived in our region. " Applied science cannot be separated from pure science." The inclusion of subjects which can be called " applied science " has a three-fold academic advantage. In the first place it is an impetus to the kind of scientific research by which knowledge is extended. In the second place, by running the practical and the theoretical together, it is educationally a sound and a profound doctrine. " To see, to think, and to act are very different things, and one advantage a science training has over others lies in the way in which all these powers are made to work together " ; the hand, the eye, and the ear are trained as more effective instruments of the mind. Lastly, through the recognition of applied science, the University gains the unmeasurable advantage of closer contact with real life. In universities, there are some who " may look back with regret on the days when the student could shut himself up within the walls of his house, and live amongst his books and instruments unconcerned with what went on outside, and careless whether his work would bear any fruit or none ". " There is at present little room for such men in our Universities ", and if we regret the passing of the old epoch, " we must take consolation in the thought that many lives were wasted in unproductive retirement, which might have been beneficial to mankind if forced into more useful exertion by that outside influence " which comes from the surge of real life. Hence Schuster summarily enunciates his academic policy. " On all grounds, therefore, must we hail with pleasure the inroads which Applied Science is making into our universities. I have shown that the separation of pure and applied science is an artificial one, rendered necessary, however, by the growth of theoretical knowledge ; it should be our endeavour to minimise the dangers of that separation, on the one hand by giving practical men a sound theoretical training, but on the other hand also by keeping theory in touch with practical requirements."

Schuster's insight and commonsense prevented him from being tied up by mainly verbal, or, in other cases, by entirely metaphysical difficulties concerning the distinction between pure and applied science. He grasped the fundamental fact of human nature that the proper education for any person is through the particular bodies of knowledge which have particular and direct reference to that person. The scientific frame of mind and the scientific technique was the same in seeking a solution to any natural problem, whether the problem be classed as purely scientific or as one of applied science. The spate of argument and verbal jugglery which seeks to divide science into two sorts of science, pure and applied (instead of recognising that, of course, there can be two different motives in manipulators of scientific method, that of the one operating freely, and that of the other operating under conditions extraneously imposed) is simply the scientists' form of the arts heresy of knowledge for its own sake. Even in its " purest " form knowledge is useless unless it has awakened in the man who knows it an intimate sense for the power, the beauty and the structure of ideas : and what can be conceived of as more useful than such a sense to gratify the highest desires of the human spirit ?

Tout's partnership in the ideals of Schuster was even more intimate than Ward's with Roscoe's. Ward was complementary to Roscoe ; Tout applied himself to developing the Arts studies, not merely as a balancing complement to scientific ones, but as a part, with science, of a common academic body, integrated in a common objective with a common method of pursuing that objective.   Before coming to Manchester, Tout's task at Lampeter had been to infuse vigour and imaginative force into a theological and arts college which was exhibiting signs of inanition.   Coming to Manchester he saw how the activities of its science departments were generating unsuspected energies in a new academic organism.   He realised that the vigour of the scientific departments was inspired by their aim to extend knowledge.   He acclaimed this objective as the really energising element in an academic community and devoted himself to adapting it to the studies pursued in a Faculty of Arts.   It is not easy to define which qualities in the all-round greatness of Tout's personality determined the general pattern of his academic policy.   Learned as he was, his humanity was greater than his scholarship.   Forcible and cogent as was his thinking, his intuitions were profounder than his thoughts, and his prejudices often sounder than the arguments by which he rationalised them.   His impassioned belief in the methods of technical historical research as the highest academically educational instrument was based probably on his realisation as a teacher that if you are teaching the things which you yourself are exploring, your teaching arouses imaginative participation by your pupils.   The educational generalisation, however, of the technical method of research as a discipline in itself, without regard to its content, is argumentatively less convincing : and the reasons submitted in defence of the discipline as one with general validity, though primarily devised for students who are to be historians in a professional or a semi-professional way, are even more speculative.   Indeed, the absolute stress which Tout laid on the training in method for research as the governing plan of an Honours School was probably the outcome of other of his deeper intuitions, of his humanity and of his sense of duty to the institution of which he was a part.   He exalted research as the controlling law, and yet he never forgot that " man cannot earn his living by historical research—at least not in this country—and one has to consider the practical question how graduates in history earn their living as well as how much good work they turn out ".   Moreover, he was a member of a new university which had already secured recognition of high status in scientific studies.   His immediate duty was to see that Manchester's Faculty of Arts was recognised as a place of learning and scholarship entitled to full academic prestige. Manchester in its Arts studies was to be as good as any other university in the way in which university goodness was traditionally assessed, that is, by its output in scholarship. He undoubtedly made it so. If the particular formulation of values as he saw them seems at times questionable, one thing is certain. Whatever calculated theory of action Tout had adopted as a planned method, in practice it would have operated as an invigorating stimulus, for Tout's temperament and character mattered much more than his system. These comments are not here set down in belittlement of Tout. He was one of the most powerful, the most creative, the most salutary academic influences anyone can hope to meet; the comments ventured here are only recorded in the fear that when his own formulation of a university policy is read in cold print by one who never knew him, the immensity of his share in making modern universities, Manchester, and all the other Redbricks which have followed its shape, may not be apparent. Everything he says has to be assessed in the light of his own description of his general philosophy; he was " a conservative for radical reasons ". In his university policy he was a leader of all progressive movements, but, if called upon to defend them, he tended to appeal in the traditional phraseology of orthodoxy and to urge the changes as merely next steps in a demonstrable process of continuity.

He had formulated a definite picture of the relative values of university activities and, especially, of the priority amongst them which must be the ultimate criterion for judging the value of the others.

" History and modern experience show that a real University is something much less mechanical than a federation of teachers for the sake of giving degrees of a uniform quality and seeing that their colleagues do not cheat in favour of their own pupils. The true Universities are something much more than this. They are associations of scholars and students, teachers and taught, whose ideal end is to make the life of learning and science possible, whose greatest function is the advancement of learning, and whose rank in the academic hierarchy ultimately depends upon the contributions made by their members to the sum of human knowledge and the enlargement of the range of human thought. Side by side with this supreme function is the function of education. This involves not only teaching, but also the contact of mind and mind, of teacher and student, without as well as within the lecture room, and living as far as may be the common social as well as the common

THE COLLEGE OF TECHNOLOGY, *circa* 1905.

G

intellectual, life. Only a minority of those instructed can aspire to add to knowledge, and for their sake, as well as for its own, the University must seek to impress itself upon the life of this community, and must be in touch with the practical as well as the academic side of things. It must not refuse to admit into its curriculum subjects which are deemed as useful, but, rather, making all knowledge its province, must see that whatever it studies is studied with academic thoroughness and method." The ultimate scale of values is categorically stated. " The true measure of academic progress is the share which the university takes in the advancement of knowledge, and the part which it plays in training its alumni in original investigation." Hence, even more important than its honours schools is a university's post-graduate and research work.

Tout found, of course, that the application of the ideal of research to education had been much more extensively developed in experimental science than in the arts subjects. Hence he deliberately set himself to demonstrate that the way of raising the level of the academic study of history (and, by implication, of other arts subjects,) in this country is " to follow more closely the methods by which British exponents of the physical sciences have made their mark ". He was, in fact, endeavouring to change history from an amateur to a professional regimen. To many, history is but " an agreeable distraction : to some it is still philosophy and morality teaching by examples ; to others, the school of statesmanship ; to others, an incitement to patriotism ; to some a catalogue of human error, to others, the record of great men ; to some an argument for change, and to others, a reason for conservatism. Any historian who has anything to say will try to say it as well as he can, so that history often becomes a vehicle of high art as literature. All these are perfectly natural and desirable functions of history in their respective ways : but they emphasise results to the exclusion of the processes by which history is studied. For us, professional historians, who are only by accident preachers, prophets, politicians, or men of letters, history must be organised knowledge of the past. Our methods, then, must necessarily be the methods of the observational sciences, and we require as much training in the technique of our craft as any other skilled worker."

The adaptation of the research methods of the scientists to the problems of arts research was the ideal which Tout adopted. In developing his policy, he may seem so intent on increasing the sum of human knowledge as to push into the background the other academic objective he had indicated, namely, the enlargement of the range of human thought ; he may also seem too ready to assume that the " observational " quality of the scientific method—which a faculty of arts can imitate only within its own limits—is synonymous with the " experimental " method, which is largely unavailable to arts studies, if not largely irrelevant.   His whole doctrine of an Arts Faculty, may, indeed, seem to obscure the major difference between physical science and humane learning, namely, that one seeks the law behind the facts of physical nature and the other seeks for values in human judgments.   But Tout himself was never guilty of being deluded by these merely verbal shortcomings in his formula.   If anything, he over-estimated the capacity of his disciples to grasp his doctrine ; and not infrequently to-day one finds a mere technique exalted as a science and the accumulation of bare facts hailed as a presentation of history. Tout was perpetually proud of the claim that he had helped to raise history from antiquated pedantry and literary elegance to the dignity of a science ; but he never forgot the object of the science, the effort to reconstruct some aspect of the past as a living social organism.   After all, the essential stages to progress in his own chosen field of research, the Middle Ages, were the finding, the sorting, the classification, and the interpretation of original manuscript material : processes as technical and scientific as those of the geologist with his rocks.   But Tout's relics were not rocks ; they were the relics of human beings : and the vivid humanity of Tout resuscitated them imaginatively.   This was his particular way of identifying teaching with research, and if perhaps he thought that this admirable result was due to his method rather than to his personal genius, others knew the true cause.

Apart from the specific articles of Tout's doctrine about the intellectual methods of academic studies, humane and scientific, or scientific and humane at once, he had a large view of the scope of university studies, and a zealous belief in linking the University with city and county at all practicable points.   In his own department, he encouraged the study of local history ; even more he extended its traditional area by instituting a chair of Economic History, the first in England and eminently at home in Manchester.   Moreover, he brought to it George Unwin, a man in whom superb mastery of the appropriate techniques of scholarship was always nothing but an instrument in the service of humanity's well-being, a man who, just out of his wealth of human kindness, opened up new lines of historical enquiry to make history serve in the search for the greater good of mankind. He himself was more of a social philosopher than an historian in the traditional sense; for him, the social aspect of history was vastly more important than the political, and even more than the economic. Indeed, even more than a social philosopher, Unwin was a social evangelist. His recurrent text was that men are linked in spiritual communion, not by legal regulation, but by the sense of belonging to this or that community (or to many communities) which have grown within society through workshop, profession, club, or church. In these the real brotherhood of man was a personal experience. An unforgettable memory of Unwin goes back to 3rd August, 1914. He, and others including myself, were assisting in a Workers' Educational Association summer school at Bangor, North Wales. I met him, at midmorning, hastening through the streets with his little gladstone bag. Being asked where he was going, he replied, " To Manchester: to stop the war." It is a further instance of Tout's sense of relative values in scholarship and of his large-mindedness that he brought Unwin to Manchester University; for Unwin's politics were anathema to Tout. But Tout saw how much Unwin had to give to history and to Manchester. Long before the opportunity to establish a chair of Economic History had occurred, Tout had supported the establishment of a Faculty of Economics and Commerce no less ardently than he participated in setting up a Faculty of Theology. In due course he was a main force in the establishment, by co-operation with the city, of the Faculty of Technology. He sought to link with the University all kindred organisations engaged in tasks similar to those of the University, the theological colleges, the endowed libraries, the training colleges and the secondary schools, and the organisations seeking to provide adult education for working men. Through all such channels as these he saw how a university, in itself a living organism, could quicken its pulse and renew its vigour by participating in the life-stream of its native place and people.

Trying dispassionately, and in retrospect, to track to their source the various currents of Tout's academic energies, and, of course, leaving out of count what was in fact the fountain-head of all he did, the immense richness of his human personality, one can see his academic life as a simple pattern of service to his idea of scholarship. Scholarship, to him, was an instrument by which all that survived from the past could be made authentically accessible to the present, and by which hitherto unconsidered or undiscovered survivals could be tracked down and put in their proper

SIR HENRY A. MIERS, VICE-CHANCELLOR 1915–1926

place in the body of organised and authenticated historic fact. The rigid orthodoxy of his conception of scholarship was invaluable to the Owens which was to become Manchester : for, without question, a university's first task is to earn the reputation of integrity in scholarship ; and scholarship must always be the primary and the final criterion of university values. Tout looked for, and seized on, all opportunities which were offered in Manchester for the development of scholarship. In the first place, his dedication to scholarship, coupled with his sense of the world, led him to see plainly that whereas the scholar proves his scholarship mainly by writing books, the greater service to scholarship which a professor can render to it is to be measured, not by the number of his own books, but by the number of pupils in whom he has instilled the spirit and the technique for producing scholarly contributions of their own. Almost all medieval historians of to-day sat closely or remotely at Tout's feet.

Tout's rôle not only in recording history, but in producing historians, determined some of his major activities in Manchester. One need only recall a few of them. He grasped at every opportunity to increase the material available in Manchester for historical research, and to ensure a stream of the right kind of student to make use of the material. To secure the material, he planned an ordered development of the University library and seized on such opportunities for extending its resources as was provided by the purchase of Freeman's library. Furthermore he initiated a scheme of departmental libraries, and built up for his own subject a collection of departmental books which permitted the teaching of history to be a course of instruction in the handling and interpretation of " original documents ". But even more important, he saw the importance to Manchester University of the inauguration of the John Rylands Library. He was a governor of it from the outset, and, later, its chairman of governors. His counsel enabled the John Rylands to become a repository of the primary documents by which many phases of medieval life can be still further illuminated : to Tout, the collection was the indispensable body of material through which he could train young historians in the method and rationale of their historical scholarship.

To provide these young historians, he built up an honours school of history. It owed, no doubt, something to the idea of an Oxford historical " schools " or a Cambridge tripos. But it went beyond them ; it was constructed as a nice equipoise between the calls of education and the necessities of research. Tout may perhaps have pushed research training a little too prominently into the undergraduate course. But he was always fully conscious that research was a post-graduate activity and presumed an adequate prior training in an undergraduate school. Hence he sought means of getting to Manchester the kind of graduate student who could be trained to join this body of historical researchers. He persuaded the University to subsidise graduate scholarships. He wanted, moreover, to bring into his graduate school promising historians whose first degree had been taken elsewhere. He persuaded Council to offer scholarships which would make it possible, not only for a Manchester graduate, but for an Oxford or Cambridge graduate, to join his school. In doing this, he was adapting to English circumstance what he had seen to be the productive way of American universities. Long before he came to Manchester, a few valuable post-graduate scholarships had been endowed in Owens College. Some, such as the Langton Fellowship (endowed 1878), were clearly for tenure immediately after graduation ; but one in particular, the Berkeley Fellowship, which was endowed in 1881 and continued until 1895, had been founded on the American plan as it was practised in the graduate school of Johns Hopkins University at Baltimore. The donor of this endowment, anonymous at the time, but on his death in 1897 revealed as W. Seaton Brown, a London friend of Thomas Ashton, was specific in the purposes which he wished to endow. " These fellowships are mainly intended for young men, original investigators in science and literature or in training for professorships, i.e. intended for teachers of the highest grade rather than for men who propose adopting any of the learned professions (excepting, perhaps, the medical) as a means of livelihood." (The donor added—" I don't care to help on young men either for the church or for the law—ninety-nine times in a hundred the world would be no poorer if they did fail.") These Berkeley Fellowships were available for the first five years of Tout's occupancy of the history chair in Manchester ; and though no historical student secured a Berkeley Fellowship in those five years, Tout was obviously influenced by the existence of such subsidies for research, since it opened up possibilities of a graduate school for the training of researchers and professors on the model of the progressive universities of the United States. Hence Tout was perpetually seeking to increase the means of subsidising the research student, and especially those who came from other universities.

His scheme for building up a graduate school (or in more familiar English phrase, a research department) led to his active interest in the setting up, towards the end of the European war of 1914–18, of a new English University degree, the doctorate of philosophy, Ph.D. The general intention of the whole plan was clear. From 1900 to 1914 there had been from England and from America a steady stream of post-graduate students to the universities of Germany. It was indeed an established academic habit ; when I graduated at Leeds in 1911, and was awarded a fellowship, my Oxford-Balliol professor insisted, and I have never regretted it, that I should go to Germany and not to Oxford. So when the war was coming to an end the English universities, and especially the scientists in them, saw a means of developing their own post-graduate activities and of attracting to them the Americans who had previously gone to Germany. They were not trying to capitalise a world situation. Indeed, when the subject was first raised in Manchester in January, 1917, it was in a document submitted by the American Association of University professors, which urged that Great Britain should take such a step. Acting on this prompting, Manchester devised its plans to meet the situation. Nothing less than a doctorate would be a sufficient bait. Hence the institution of the Ph.D., the doctorate in philosophy, where philosophy has the old German and Scottish connotation which comprises all and every component of knowledge. For Tout, the historian, this was a great opportunity ; for medieval history necessitates a technique of research in which the methods of the scientist can be most easily accommodated to the purposes of the historian. It was a subject in which principles and techniques of research could be taught in a fashion closely similar to the practice in scientific subjects. So Tout, in the interests of scholarship as the historian saw scholarship, became the prime mover on the Arts side for the setting up of the new degree. Whatever may have been the less valuable results of the institution of the doctorate in philosophy, there is no doubt that it has provided a very useful instrument in the carrying forward of Tout's major objective, the development of historical scholarship.

Of course, Tout saw that scholarship only acquires value when its findings are accessible to those who can evaluate them. Hence the publication of scholarly findings is a necessity in the development of scholarship as an instrument for extending knowledge. From very early in its history Owens College had formed the habit of publishing such significant lectures, mainly inaugural lectures, as it thought desirable. But each publication of this kind was a separate venture, undertaken and paid for by the college as the occasion arose. In 1886, Council authorised the publication of a volume, edited by Milnes Marshall (the professor whose tragic death in a Lakeland climbing accident cost the University one of its most progressive members), which was to be a first item in a series of " studies from the biological laboratories of Owens College ". In 1891, the Council similarly sponsored a volume of Physiological Studies to be edited by Professor Stirling. Tout, of course, was one of the main forces, indeed for a time the only Arts representative, on the Publications Committee. But when Manchester University became independent in 1903, it immediately addressed itself, and largely at Tout's instigation, to considering the scope of its own Publications Committee. A scheme was devised by which Sherratt & Hughes, the Manchester booksellers, printers, and publishers, should become printers and publishers to the University. The decision served to make one of the partners of Sherratt & Hughes, J. D. Hughes (in whose Cross Street underground storehouse of secondhand books had congregated men of letters whose national and international fame was recognised and younger unknown ones eager to meet and chat with those who had already achieved the reputation to which they in their turn were aspiring), a life-long friend of the University and a man knowledgeable in the ways by which a young university lecturer could get the out-of-the-way books he wanted and at the price he could afford to pay. The association with Sherratt & Hughes as publishers to the University lasted until 1913. In the meantime, and all the time Tout's was the effective motive force, Council had authorised the appointment of a full-time secretary to what was still called the University Publications Committee. H. M. McKechnie, experienced in the business of commercial publication, was appointed to the post in 1912. Almost at once the Publications Committee recommended the setting up of a University Printing Press. Council demurred, and taking the situation all in all, and at this moment fresh from hearing opinions personally expressed by directors of University Presses in the United States of America, one is inclined to think that Council was right. Some change in the organisation, however, was effected. To handle the distribution business of the Press, it was thought good to transfer the function of Publishers to the University Press from Sherratt & Hughes to Longmans Green & Co., with the hope that through them, not only a more general

English, but a wider European and American area might be covered. On 27th October, 1915, the Publications Committee was authorised by Council to name itself the University Press Committee. Its policy was a strictly academic one. As a publishing body, it sought to persuade Council that more and more resources should be placed at its disposal to enable it to publish works of scholarship which could not possibly secure the interest of a commercial publisher. Its own plan was to assist young Manchester researchers, students or lecturers, to get their research work into print, and so provide themselves with the evidences by which one side of their academic worth could be estimated. It was Tout's plan, and Tout's consistent policy. Of course, his own field of study lent itself much more readily to the production of doctoral theses by researchers beginning their career than do other humanist, but non-historical, subjects. But by building up the Manchester University Press, and by making it an instrument for publishing books of historical research, Tout fixed Manchester firmly on the scholars' map of Europe as the University which had produced, amongst other publications, a series of historical books and monographs unsurpassed by those of any other University Press. The Press now stands on its own feet as publisher; it withdrew from the arrangement with Longmans, and now continues as an independent publishing body, becoming more and more widely known in Europe and in the United States of America. The groundwork was devised by Tout, and laid practically by H. M. McKechnie. It is for the present and the immediate future to reap the harvest which they sowed.

Behind all this academic activity, Tout maintained a consciousness of the value of intimate association between city and university. It led him to take active part in the agitation, from 1900 until success came, for the splitting of the federal university and the recognition of an independent University of Manchester. It was a topic put forcibly by Samuel Alexander in the public press in 1902, when he stressed the need for " a sense of the organic connection of a university with its city and district ". " Call it by whatever name you will—civic or communal sentiment, or, as I have said, the sentiment of organic connection—it is the feeling that a university meets the desires of the people for it, and that it is strong according as they take interest and pride in the extension of its influence and in the distinction of its members. From another point of view, it is the sense that academic work, the life of the teacher, and the learner, and the investigator, is not something remote from daily interests

but is a form of citizenship." Through the closeness of its relationship
to its province, a " university can take its proper place as the crown of the
educational system of the district ". Alexander, professor of Philosophy
from 1893 to 1924, was nearly contemporary with Tout : and he publicly
asserted that it was from Tout that he learnt so much about academic
ideals. In 1931, already recognised as one of the world's greatest creative
philosophers, honoured, too, by the Order of Merit, he set down his
considered faith about the nature and function of a university, a faith
which he had reached during his thirty years in Manchester University.
Here follows the article he then wrote.

CHAPTER VI

THE ALEXANDER VERSION OF THE MANCHESTER IDEA

*(An article by Samuel Alexander published in " The Political Quarterly ",
September, 1931, and reproduced here by permission)*

I SHOULD describe a university as an association or corporation of
scholars and teachers engaged in acquiring, communicating, or
advancing knowledge, pursuing in a liberal spirit the various sciences
which are a preparation for the professions or higher occupations of
life. The omission of any part of this description would convey a false
impression of what a university is. It does not exist only for acquiring
or communicating the higher branches of knowledge, but for extending
them as well; and it does not only pursue the sciences for their own
sake, but, so far as the larger part of its members are concerned, pursues
them in preparation for the professions. I had almost said that the purpose
of a university was to prepare for the professions, and I should be ready
to defend this, provided that the qualifying words, " in a liberal spirit ",
are not merely not omitted but emphasised. Without such emphasis, it is
safer to say not that its purpose or object is the professions, which may
appear too utilitarian, but that it does in fact prepare for the professions
by pursuing the sciences on which those professions are founded. In fact
it is impossible to divorce the work of a university from its practical issues
in life. A university is not, and never has been, a society of persons cultivating the sciences for their own sake, in the sense that that is its purpose.
That is rather its method than its purpose. A society whose purpose is
the cultivation of science is without pupils and is an academy like the
Royal Society or the British Academy. As a matter of fact, universities
tend more and more to take over and include the work of academies. The
larger part of the advancement of science is done in the universities, and

academies tend to become societies of persons whose selection is a distinction awarded for work done and an encouragement to pursue it further. Academies, with their avowed limitation to the advancement of knowledge, recede accordingly in comparison with the universities. One common theory of the university, not put into practice, is that the chief object of the professor is the work of discovery and his functions as a teacher are subsidiary and secondary. This exaggeration has happily not taken root amongst ourselves, not through any virtue of our own but because our universities are not yet developed enough to insist on the advancement of knowledge as a necessary part of their existence.

In our own day and in this country, if I were asked to point to the most distinctive feature of university work, I should say it was the inclusion of technology, and that inclusion is the best key to the understanding of the real business of a university as we conceive it at present. Even the older universities have agriculture and engineering. The last is a school of old standing, for instance, in Manchester, but now all branches of technology are included there and at Leeds. The practice of Germany is different, where the higher technical school, the *technische Hochschule*, remains independent and is not included in the university. I gather that the wisdom of this is not unquestioned. At the same time, in Prussia, a doctor's degree is given, Ing.D., Doctor of Engineering. And besides technology there are now included in our universities other than purely technical sciences : industrial science which prepares for the higher walks of commerce, administration, and the training for the teacher's profession, not merely in the subjects which he has to teach, but in the science of his special profession of teaching.

We are here face to face with the secret of the university. It is, in all these studies, not only the older and well-established academic subjects but the newer more obviously professional subjects, in each subject to pursue its science. The word science is here used, not in its unfortunate restriction to the natural and mathematical sciences, but in its comprehensiveness in which it includes Arts. Science means, first, the study of the rational principles underlying each subject or art, and second, establishing relations between one subject and another, generalising or distinguishing, which process is the beginning of philosophy. It was this latter function which absorbed almost entirely the mind of Newman when he delivered his famous lectures on " The Idea of a University ", as part of the attempt to found a Roman Catholic University in Ireland.

SIR WALTER H. MOBERLY, Vice-Chancellor 1926–1934
(*From the portrait by James Gunn*)

My concern is not with this, but only to note that it is this systematic and deliberate effort to understand by principles, to discover the reasons of facts, instead of merely acquiring familiarity with a subject of knowledge, or merely acquiring technical skill in the handling of a certain material, which makes the difference between elementary and higher education; and that university and secondary education themselves differ, not so much in kind, as in the relatively greater open-eyedness with which the object is pursued. There are all manners of causes which prevent this clear separation of the university and the secondary school—in England the backward condition of the schools, which means that students have to occupy part of their academic years with work which in France and Germany is done in the lycées or the gymnasia. Such backwardness is a serious impediment to carrying out at the university the true spirit of academic life which is that of independence of mind; the student is still too much of a schoolboy, has still too much to acquire with help before he can learn to dispense with teaching and be content with guidance.

I need not linger upon the topic of the general scientific character of science. Nor need I offer more than a very few examples. The subjects of the faculty of " science " illustrate most clearly what I have said; although the natural sciences differ very much among themselves, in their age, and in the character of their material, which requires in some cases a much larger occupation with description and history as distinct from experiment and generalisation. I take examples rather from practical subjects such as engineering and medicine. The first is clearly an application of dynamical and statistical principles which have to be studied if a man is to be an engineer with intelligence; and the materials he deals with as in building a bridge, and the methods devised for testing their strength or elasticity, are studied not to acquire facility in dealing with these materials directly, as the steelwright or the shipwright do, but in relation to the physical principles to be applied. In medicine the academic purpose is doubtless obscured, in this oldest of the academic disciplines, by the length of time that has to be spent in getting to know the body. But more and more such mere knowledge as in anatomy which is the necessary familiarity that has to be acquired with a new subject-matter and corresponds to schooling in ordinary subjects; more and more such mere familiarity is illuminated with comparative study and with the vital knowledge of function. What makes the physician or surgeon is to know the importance of any one part of the body for the integral life, and his purely medical knowledge is inspired with physiology. I say nothing of the other sciences which are propædeutic to the more special scientific knowledge of the kind of animal and mind the medical man has to handle in his profession. They are themselves of value in so far as they generate in him the scientific love (Plato would have called it so) of penetrating more and more into the reasons of his procedure in surgery or of his reliance on the physiological influences of the drugs he uses in medicine or the psychological influences of the persuasions he uses in curing a diseased mind.

As a last example I take the Arts, which a university treats not as arts to practise, but as arts to be understood. Thus school makes us familiar with the use of our own language and with some of its literature. But the science of English literature teaches us to understand its causes, its connection with the times at which it was produced, the place of any work in the history of the whole ; and having learned to enjoy Shakespeare in a good school, we can follow the guidance of a critic like Mr. A. C. Bradley and understand Shakespeare's æsthetic effect by learning with what subtle minuteness his words can be analysed. It is not Shakespeare's deliberate intentions which are thus laid bare but the causes affecting his mind as he worked with the artist's intuition of what was fitting to his characters and situations. For the artist is one thing ; the man who understands him is another, and he is the critic. Now one does not need to go to a university to enjoy English literature, but one does in order to enjoy it with understanding.

I need not pursue further illustration to convince you that the same thing is true in applied chemistry, in history, in architecture, in brewing which is studied in Birmingham, or in music. What makes the study in all these cases academic is its liberal spirit which can be cultivated as well, though perhaps with greater difficulty in the attainment, in natural science and technology as in the subjects such as literature and in particular ancient literature or the moral sciences which used to monopolise the name of liberal subjects. Liberality is a spirit of pursuit, not a choice of subject. But I desire to prevent your supposing that the spirit of science and of liberality, because it is a spirit and not the material, can be acquired without the labour of attaining knowledge. There is much affected depreciation of knowledge, as if the accumulation of information were worthless. Let us clear our minds of that cant, and recognise that Dr. Johnson was right when he said that " all knowledge is of itself of some value ". But it is true that knowledge which cannot be used is of little value. Now to use knowledge we have to learn its reasons, to understand it ; but we cannot learn to use it without the hard labour of acquiring it. Only he can leave others to acquire, and himself direct the understanding of it, who has learnt himself what the method of understanding is from his own labour in some particular field.

I do not know the history of the phrase " the liberal arts ". Partly the phrase implies imperfectly a contrast, to which I shall presently return, between the arts and the crafts of life. Partly certain subjects have been raised into eminence because they have been thought to be the best preparation for public life or for what was called in a less democratic age the education of gentlemen. The classical languages and literatures were specially singled out, and the reason is that at one time Latin was the ordinary language of cultivated intercourse, not only internationally but also within the nation. Partly it was that these languages contained the finest or some of the finest works of literature and were the key to understanding the law and religion and generally the civilisation of Europe, and moreover embodied, and especially Greek, the history and thought of a people of rare gifts. Those claims still remain and it would argue a spirit not of science but of levity to dismiss these studies as no longer having the right to their old importance. What I have been endeavouring to show is that their liberalising effect lies in the spirit with which they are pursued, not as accomplishments merely which add to the grace of life, as undoubtedly they do, but as opening the mind to insight into human affairs and things.

Apart from these accidental or historical associations of the phrase, "a liberal education", there is a real reason why academic study, if it is true to its aim, deserves the name of liberal, as being the study of the sciences in the widest sense. It sets us free from the routine which besets the practice of any craft, it saves knowledge from being merely an acquisition or merely useful, animates it with reason and gives it life and zest. I spoke advisedly of craft. For the difference is the same as obtains between craft, which by itself is mere skill and is bent on producing a product of utility, and art which makes the product beautiful. The craftsman, who is content to be nothing else or is unable to be so, is deadened by service to utility and may be and often is replaced by a machine. The liberal craftsman, even if he is unable for want of special gift to ennoble his craftsmanship by art and originality, yet strives for perfection in his work, or ennobles it with the delight he takes in the exercise of his skill. Lately Sir Francis Goodenough has been applying this truth to ordinary business, and been pleading for the " romance ", as he calls it, which might be cultivated in buying and selling, the delight in it which might redeem it from drudgery, by making it a means to an end beyond the mere doing of it, and might create happiness out of occupations of utility adopted for the necessary purpose of securing daily bread. What art or passion is to the workman, science is to the knowledge which is required for the practice of the professions, which, however little we may like to think so, are as much craft as the work of the artisan—the craft of the surgeon or doctor, of the lawyer, of the teacher or the architect. So far as these are mere crafts they may be practised with the dullness of routine or may be animated by art or passion. But these higher crafts, for which academic studies are preliminary, have in a higher degree than the lower ones the advantage that the practice of them depends on a previous cultivation of knowledge. Now knowledge may be ossified into the rule of intelligent habit, into mere routine. The habit of reason which is science keeps it alive, and even if a professional man can carry no further the science he has learnt, can at most keep himself abreast of new knowledge and new methods, he has acquired at the university, or should have acquired, the spirit of science which liberalises knowledge by keeping it free of mere habit and utility.

A university thus trains its members to perform their craft with liberation from the mere doing of it, because it supplies them with the enlightening quest of reason. All our studies therefore are pursued, not without regard to their utility for life, but not for the sake of their utility. What the university seeks to provide is the command of a subject, afterwards to be applied, which will make the application worthy of a free man. Such education may justly be called liberal. It is idle to say to a student, do not think of the future, of what you are going to do to earn your bread and play your part in life. But my advice to a student would be, choose your career, primarily from inclination, or if there is no determinate inclination, or the choice is settled by necessity or convenience, then by the advice of persons whom you trust ; but having done so surrender yourself to the one immediate end of mastering your subject, which is the condition of the future ability which brings with it not only mere success but what is worth much more, happiness.

Hitherto I have been speaking of the university from the point of view of the scholars. It is time to turn to the teachers and their methods.

It goes without saying, that the methods of training must, or rather should, be such as to stimulate in each subject the capacity for independence of mind on the part of every student. The extent to which that independence may be expected to reach will depend upon the subject and upon the student. A greater achievement may be asked from a young man or woman in a language or history than perhaps in physics or philosophy. But whatever the student's capacity may be, he can be expected to exercise his own judgment and not merely repeat the words of his teacher or his textbook, and if unable to make small advances of his own, to give an intelligent account of the work of others and indicate its value. While, on the other hand, the methods must be such that the better student may prosecute, under the guidance of the teacher, some piece of research, however limited, and become qualified, if his tastes lead him to the scholarly life, to carry on the work of investigation or at least to acquire the mastery of a science which may make him a live teacher of others. How far we are from having attained this ideal in the British universities it is needless to insist.

Lest we be too much exalted by achievements like the late T. F. Tout's school of history at Manchester, let us remember that such schools of investigation are the accepted and regular standard of German and, I believe, of French Universities, and are remarkable amongst ourselves only because of their rarity. Before they become usual we shall doubtless need to wait till by the acceleration of higher education in the secondary schools, the universities are fed with students able to profit in their degree by such methods. Social and educational conditions alike make such attainment impossible for the present. Perhaps too they make difficult for some time obedience to a corollary which follows immediately from this statement of the academic method, that at least in the younger universities, far less stress should be laid on lectures and far more on work in laboratories or, what corresponds to it in the arts, in libraries and private reading, so that in the first place students should be encouraged to help themselves, and the teacher, in the second place, be set free from the burden of overlecturing and be free to help students where he best can by guidance in the student's individual efforts.

For the teacher is a vital member of the association which makes a university and it is to him that it looks for the business of advancing the

H

boundaries of knowledge.   Should the teachers be in the main investigators or in the main teachers ?   The answer is that the question raises an unreal antithesis, for to speak generally, the academic teacher can teach the spirit of science only if he himself embodies it and is an investigator, and on the other hand it does him good as an investigator to be a teacher : by helping others on the way of reason and discovery, he clears his own mind and gets light to illuminate his own path.   On the one hand in his case, the absurd saying " who drives fat oxen must himself be fat " becomes not absurd but true.   How shall he imbue others with " the rapture of the forward view " in knowledge who does not himself take the forward view ?   On the other hand, the scientific man (and I remind you that science means every kind of knowledge ordered and vitalised by reason) does not stand apart from his contemporaries or from his juniors.   He learns wisdom from the mouths of babes ; and if he is to hand on the torch, and science is only kept alive through tradition from one generation to another, he must teach his successors how to hold it. Nor is his obligation limited to the training of other investigators.   He is not only a professor but a man, and the greater his gift, the more urgent is the appeal to him to communicate it.   " Wie viel bist du von andern unterschieden ? " Goethe asks of himself; how much do you differ from others ?

The unreality of the question being recognised, we remodel the question into the form, what is the first duty of the academic teacher ? and the answer is not doubtful.   It is himself to investigate and to inspire others with that spirit, in all its due degrees of appropriateness.   But in practice the answer is not so easy to apply.   There are two kinds of scholars who are exceptional.   One kind is the great investigator who cannot teach more than an exceptional few whom he inspires.   To the general run of students he makes no appeal and, useless as a general teacher, he is thought to be useless to a university.   He is, in fact, the salt of a university (one of the most eminent men in this place is before my mind), provided he is not too numerous.   For as a dish cannot be composed of condiments, neither can a university consist of great investigators who cannot teach—Willard Gibbses and Kelvins and Osborne Reynoldses.   On the other hand a university condemns itself to smallness and sterility which cannot afford to have such.   There is the other exceptional type of men who, being really full of the scientific spirit, do not themselves discover but are admirable teachers.   A university cannot afford to be without such, but dare not have them too many. Sometimes a man is a born teacher but though he does not himself discover has the gift of setting others to discover. Who shall measure his value or do other than welcome him? Perhaps the only conclusions we can draw are that the ideal teacher is at once investigator and teacher (I have known one teacher at once a great mathematical investigator and a consummate teacher), and happy the university whose teachers are in the main of this kind; and that the great teacher who does not investigate is more worth a university's having than one who investigates, not because he wants to, but because he is expected to do so. For a man when he is young may begin by desiring to investigate; and, disappointing himself, may discover that his strength lies in teaching, and his work may be invaluable. The statement sometimes made that teaching is but an interruption in the proper work of a professor is therefore to be rejected unconditionally, though it may be useful for us in England to remember what it contains of reasonableness. It is perhaps not intended seriously and certainly not practised, and the real lesson of it is what was said before, that the most useful teaching of a professor is not always the lecture but the guidance of students in laboratory or learned investigations.

One thing at least is certain, that a university fails in one of its essential functions which is not so equipped in sufficiency of teachers, or in the arrangements of its teaching, as to allow time and room for, and to encourage by all possible helps and incitements, the prosecution by its teachers of investigation in their sciences. The chief obstacle is the overteaching of students, which is a glaring defect of our English universities in general, and it sins in two ways against the ideal of a university. It tends to continue in the university the methods of the school, treating as still a schoolboy the student who should be rather trained to exercising his own freedom of mind, to make the best of himself by his own efforts, under advice, and to grow into his intellectual independence as an equal member of a society aiming to acquire and to promote the scientific spirit. And in spoon-feeding the student, it engrosses the time of the teacher and keeps him from prosecuting from the beginning of his academic life the work which it is his special business or profession to do. For myself, as an Oxford man and bound by every tie of affection and gratitude to her, it is painful to reflect that this is still a cardinal defect of that great university. Things have no doubt changed much for the better since Mark Pattison, in 1856, protested that Oxford was no more than a school, teaching indeed the higher branches of learning but forgetting that one part of its duty, and the part without which the rest cannot be duly performed, was the advancement of science and not its mere tradition. That second function she performs admirably, and has thrown herself with splendid enthusiasm and success into the work of popularising knowledge. But in the advancement of it by discovery she has been content, not merely to yield the place, as she has done for many years, to her sister, but even when the magnitude is considered of her resources and her numbers, and her attraction for the best material of the country, to fall behind some at least of the younger and growing universities who have not yet arrived at greatness but maintain a steady consciousness of their duty towards the advancement of science.

There is always an appearance of exaggeration in making such an accusation against a university which has had in the ranks of its teachers so many great or illustrious men. But I am thinking not of individuals in a large and splendid university, but of the general impression she leaves of not pulling her weight in the enterprise of learning. More causes have been at work than one in producing this result, upon which it would be interesting, if there were space and if I were better qualified than an outsider can possibly be, to dilate. Universities have their temperaments, and there may be some such reason why Oxford has been, at any rate in the immediate past, as Stanley said, the mother of great movements rather than of great men. Mr. Havelock Ellis, in a fascinating study of the source of British talent or genius, has pointed to the statistical fact that Oxford draws her students in the main from the west of the Pennines and from the West Country, from the peoples of Celtic stock. It is difficult, however, to believe that the romantic strain of its students, so far as it exists, should interfere so greatly with the prosecution of knowledge. And I am concerned to note rather a more obvious cause in the organisation of the University, because it admits of reform if the will is not wanting. That feature is the tutorial system which is carried at Oxford to perfection, which did the University essential service when it was introduced at a time when the University had ceased to teach its students at all, but now that the duty of teaching is well recognised, has served its turn and has become a positive evil, and in particular, in its excess, a positive obstacle to the work of investigation.

Luckily the system has taken weaker root in the newer studies of the natural sciences. But in the subjects of the older sciences, the system is

ASHBURNE HALL, TWO VIEWS

THE ARTS LIBRARY, 1937

THE TURNER DENTAL SCHOOL, 1940

rampant ; and it is to be remembered that the strength of Oxford still lies in the humane sciences. Owing to the fatal preponderance of the college over the university as a teaching institution, teaching is for the most part in the hands, not of the professors but of the college tutors and lecturers, whose time is engrossed in the excessive individual care of the students. No one would be so foolish as to overlook the merits of the system of weekly essays, the stimulus to young men from discussion with older men, its cultivation of readiness and ease in writing. From the point of view of the student it is not intercourse with tutors which is to be deprecated but the excess of it. And because the tutor is absorbed during term and in the vacation exhausted from his labour, he is not free, except by the exercise of great energy of character, to maintain his work of investigation. Naturally the output of scientific work is limited. Nor does the evil stop there. When a professor is to be chosen for the university, one or two things may happen. He may be and naturally is chosen from the ranks of the college teachers, but though set free from the exhausting work of tuition he reaches leisure at an age when he has lost the habit of investigation. The alternative is to appoint a man from the outside already distinguished as an investigator. Even he may be of comparatively little use, for the teaching of students remains in the hands of the college tutors, and the students, and in particular the more gifted ones, are not trained with an eye to possible life as a scholar. The result of this system is that the gifted student instead of being directed from the beginning to the work of investigation, chooses it, if he chooses it at all, with effort rather than because he is encouraged to do so. Thus the sacrifice of the highly gifted younger men who become college tutors to the interest of teaching students cuts off the supply of investigators at both ends. The result would be deplorable in any case, but not so much to be deplored if the excessive teaching were good for the students themselves. Upon the average student on the contrary it seems to be largely thrown away. Nor is there any sufficient evidence that the overtaught undergraduates of Oxford are better fitted for the work of life than those of Cambridge who have not had to suffer from these advantages.

I described a university in starting as a corporation or association and disregarded the happy accident by which the word has come to imply a place where all the sciences are pursued. The accident or misunderstanding is a happy one, for it is true in general that a university cannot safely or for long omit without endangering its own vitality any of the well-marked groups of the sciences. It does not follow that each university must study every member of these groups and it may be a matter of nice consideration to which subjects a particular university should pay special attention. In actual fact it is largely historical circumstances which settle the differences of universities in this respect. But the principle involved is clear and the reason of it. Knowledge is like a tree, whose one-sided growth impedes the healthy growth of the side which is retained. Lop off certain branches of the tree, and the tree suffers in what is left of it. Or to change the simile or metaphor, the university lives to cultivate the spirit of science, but that spirit is on the one hand infectious and spreads from science to science by wholesome contagion ; and on the other hand, if it is shut out from any of its larger fields of action, it returns upon itself and narrowed in its freedom generates humours and diseases, loses the warmth of amplitude and becomes petty or meticulous or in other ways artificial. Accordingly, when it was gravely proposed that a certain great university should confine itself to the human sciences, and, leaving the natural sciences to other universities, pour upon the human sciences all its resources, remaining a focus of ancient studies and neglecting the newer ones, the proposers forgot that the chief sufferer would be the human sciences themselves ; that, cut off from the animating spirit of a great new interest of knowledge, the old interest would wither and decline. The monstrous suggestion has fortunately never been adopted, but it operates still wherever the old order, pleading the expensiveness of newer studies, and, in particular, the great cost of laboratories in the physical sciences, endeavours to shut the window against the fresh air that blows from large new regions of intellectual interest.

As the features of life are more easily observed in a higher animal than in one which stands lower in the scale, the university exhibits in its most obvious character the actuating life of science. But it must be observed that the difference between the university and the school is not so much one of kind as of degree, or rather it arises from the relative maturity or immaturity of the persons undergoing the education. Plato was right when he insisted that elementary education is to be a preparation for the higher education, familiarising the mind of the child with the same things as it will recognise to be good and true when it reaches the use of reason. Still more obviously, secondary education begins with less severity the introduction to the methods of reason which are the avowed aims of academic education. There is one principle which runs through all acquirement and use of knowledge. But the instrument may be at one stage of the pupil's life imagination, warped more and more by reason ; at a later stage reason itself in a lighter vein ; still later the overt cultivation of the principles of science.

CHAPTER VII

MANCHESTER UNIVERSITY: IDEA INTO REALITY

IN the preceding pages, Samuel Alexander was not really expounding a vision of an ideal university : he was developing and interpreting what he had seen to be the trend of Manchester's experiment in university-making. He defines the underlying principles which have been, and still are, the predominant forces in directing the organic growth of Manchester University. He insists on the close interrelation of the work of discovery and that of teaching. He recognises thinking as a form of real research. Although in his article, Alexander did not develop the implications of this proposition, it is one which might have arrested the trend to think of teaching and research as two different kinds of academic activity : his proposition implies the fundamental identity of the two activities as academically intellectual processes. Every act of really learning (that is, of real learning), as distinct from mere extension by mechanical memorising, is the integration of new knowledge to the consciously or unconsciously systematised body of knowledge already in the possession of the learner. Such an act of learning is " original thinking ", though the thought it attains is new, not to the world, but only to the particular thinker of it. Yet it is research in the real sense, that is, in a sense which is educationally much more vital than the one by which nowadays research is discriminated from other mental activities. Academically to-day research seems to connote the application of intellectual (and not infrequently mechanical or even manual) processes to the examination of hitherto unused bodies of material such as newly discovered MSS., or to the experimental collision of two hitherto isolated chemical bodies so that the report of the collision will establish a new piece of factual information. Alexander's conception of research, establishing philosophy itself as a valid subject for academic research, and not merely the history of philosophy (which is amenable to the semi-scientific

techniques of historical research), is such a consummate integration of
the academic mind, however, that we are not yet ripe to adopt it. He
welcomes all knowledge as the province of a university, and finds in the
inclusion of Technology the best key to the understanding of the real
business of a modern university. He insists that what makes the study of
any subject academic is the liberal spirit with which it is pursued, for
liberality is a spirit of pursuit, not a discrimination of subject. He has a
strong conviction that knowledge which cannot be used is of little value.
In putting forward all these principles, Alexander is re-stating what is
inherent in the original idea of Owens, and is thus carrying the tradition
one stage further forward.

When Manchester University became autonomous and independent
in 1903, it began at once to seize the opportunities it now had for academic
expansion. The general direction of this expansion was to enlarge the
range of studies prosecuted within it and especially to develop those which
had direct significance for the well-being and the prosperity of the province. Independence had given Manchester the chance to modify its
academic organisation. It set up Faculties, that is, it gave constitutional
recognition to groups of related subjects. In 1903, it had five such
groups, Arts, Science, Law, Medicine and Music, and it devised a distinctive degree to be awarded in each of these groups. The groups
were now formally called Faculties, and the teachers who formed the
Board of a particular Faculty devised the regulations by which the degree
appropriate to that Faculty could be obtained. One plain sign of the
growth of the University is the multiplication of the number of its Faculties. In 1903, Manchester set up a Faculty of Theology and a Faculty of
Commerce : it is very characteristic of Manchester that the first two new
Faculties should have been precisely these two : the claims of the moment
and the consciousness of eternity simultaneously given their due recognition. By the Charter of 1903 the Faculty of Technology was instituted
and in 1914 came the Faculty of Education. Something has already been
said about the significance to our growth of the inclusion of a Faculty of
Theology. The importance of the other new Faculties is of a different
kind : they represented not, like Theology, the adoption by Manchester of
a traditional academic subject, but the expansion of the academic idea itself
by incorporating fresh, and, to a large extent, hitherto unacademic ranges of
study. But it was all part of a process of growth, not of sudden invasion.
Commerce grew slowly from what at first was a part-time chair of Political

Economy, held either by the professor of History or the professor of Philosophy or, as happened for a time, by the professor of Law. In 1898 it became an independent chair within the Faculty of Arts. The first occupant of the chair, A. W. Flux, was eager to implement the Owens purpose of educating young men intended for careers in commerce, and educating them not only in the traditional cultural sense, but in a manner by which they would become familiar with the sciences of which commerce and industry are the practical application. In 1899, following conferences with representatives of Manchester's industry and commerce, the University devised courses which could be followed either during the day or at evening sessions, and which would lead to a university certificate in commerce. Moreover, many of Manchester's better-known firms promised to give due consideration to this certificate when recruiting their staff. In 1902 an annuity of over £1,000 for ten years was presented to the University to enable it to establish scholarships in Commerce and Industry. As early as 1887 the college had received a bequest to promote the academic study of local government. So when Sydney Chapman took over the chair of Political Economy in 1901, time was ripening towards the development of the academic handling of the ideas which are the theoretic background of industrial arts, commercial practice, and of industrial and social administration. He came when the movement for an independent Manchester University was beginning to gain strength. His own experience in seeking to extend the range of his subject made the advantages of independence even more clear. In 1903, he had overcome a relatively slight opposition in Senate, and had persuaded Manchester, soon to be independent, to set up a Faculty of Commerce and Administration, which, when Manchester's autonomy was secured, could grant the degree of B.Com. An essential part of the proposal was that the degree courses were to be held at times fixed so that men engaged in commerce or in administration could attend them, that is, evening courses were to duplicate day classes. It was this part of the plan which caused federal trouble. Leeds and Liverpool objected ; so it could only be operated when Manchester was free, or at least free within the limits of regulations still in existence by which each of the northern universities can oppose (where, when and how is not, and experience demonstrates that it never need be, clear) any alterations in the regulations of the other northern universities. However, freedom came and the new Faculty began. It has since become, next to Medicine, and with Education,

SIR JOHN STOPFORD, VICE-CHANCELLOR 1934–
(*From the portrait by James Gunn*)

one of the strongest life-lines binding us as a university to the region in which we exist. Its orientation has been fluid. Beginning as a traditional and semi-mathematical approach to economics as an almost abstract science, it has seized on every opportunity to apply itself to the problems of its area. Gradually, its trend became clear. It established a second chair in what was called Social Economics ; it was first held by Henry Clay on his way eventually to become Warden of Nuffield College, Oxford, the most characteristic and the most important modern innovation devised to restore the intimate relationship of academic study and social well-being, that is, to fulfil the academic function which classics and the humane subjects provided for the world in the sixteenth century. The next stage in the development of the Faculty was inspired by Daniels. He was by nature that sort of born realist who can afford to treat himself to romantic notions. He never lost his grip on the immediate necessities of the moment. He never forgot how close to Manchester's public interest his own branch of study lay. At his instigation, the Faculty of Commerce developed, and then by establishing a professorship in the subject, canonised the pursuit of what can only be called realistic economic research, that is, the study of conditions in society and in industry as they now are, and an attempt to use such enquiries either to strengthen or to modify accepted academic dogma in those regions of thought. In the meantime, the University had been extending in other ways the social, as distinct from the economic and industrial, implications of the Faculty. It had established courses in, and certificates or diplomas for, many varieties of " social " work. The problem, however, was not easy. The social studies involve so much which scientists will not recognise as science, and which arts men will not recognise as scholarship : and when issues like that are raised in a university body, progress is bound to be deferred. In spite of this, however, the recognition of our obligation as a university to take cognisance of studies called " Social Studies " was not forgotten. John Stocks kept our obligation before us in many ways. But the full import of the group of studies, first called the Faculty of Commerce, and now called the Faculty of Economic and Social Studies, has only been realised within the last few years. Through its Clapham Committee the Government has now recognised that the Social Studies are just as much the primary technologies of the humane subjects as engineering is the primary technology of the sciences.

The establishment of the Faculty of Technology in 1903 (the Charter of 1903 authorised it, though the Faculty did not become effective until 1905) was for Manchester a natural rather than a novel development of the academic proliferation of its intellectual occupations. It was, however, more significant for the Manchester idea in a different way : it involved a direct constitutional partnership in the determination and control of certain branches of academic study, a partnership between the university on the one hand and the City Council on the other. Manchester had set up in its midst in 1827 a Mechanics' Institute, and the Mechanics' Institute was inaugurated in the belief that there is no mechanical employment and no manual art " which does not depend more or less on scientific principles ". The Institute would therefore teach what these principles were and what practical applications of them were possible. As the years went by, the Institute took on educational functions for its particular clientèle very different from those originally intended. It never forgot that primarily its principle was to " instruct the working classes in the principles of the art they practice ". This was a motive which secured financial support from many Manchester industrial sources, including that of Sir Joseph Whitworth. In 1882, at a meeting arranged by Oliver Heywood, son of Benjamin Heywood, and nephew of the James Heywood who was an original trustee of Owens College, it was proposed to raise funds to turn the Mechanics' Institute into a Technical School. So in 1883 day and evening courses in such subjects as engineering, chemistry, bleaching, dyeing and printing, were planned, and in due course were supplemented by courses in textile subjects like spinning and weaving. In 1889 the City was empowered to levy a twopenny rate for technical education. Very soon, Government provided it with other financial resources, and in 1890 Manchester City Council sent five people to the Continent to see how Europe was facing the problem of technical education in its widest sense, and to advise on the best way to educate Manchester youth in the theory or the science underlying all the arts, even up to the so-called fine arts, which were practised in the routine business life of the community. The result was a real attempt to bring into a unified scheme all the privately and municipally inspired and subsidised organisations for technical and " artistic " education. So in 1892 the Municipal Technical School and the Municipal School of Art were brought under the authority of a municipally appointed official called the Director and Secretary of Technical Instruction, who henceforward had control of the various municipally sponsored courses in which engineering, textile, civil and

railway engineering, even railway carriage building, were taught. Behind this effort was the idea that Manchester Corporation should set up a
Technological College which would compare with the Art School of
Vienna and the Polytechnikum of Zurich, institutions particularly designed
to teach the application of science and art to industry. It was, however,
the Swiss analogy which brought the municipal development into relation
with the activities of Manchester University. For the problem at Zurich
was different from that at Manchester. In Zurich science aimed at the
highest level of theoretical training; in Manchester that was already
provided at Owens College. So the Manchester technological school
saw that it should concern itself primarily with the application of this
theoretical training. In that spirit, and with a further reinforcement of
its objectives by modifications consequent on a deputation it sent to the
United States, the city decided to build new quarters for the Technical
School and decided also that the name of it should be changed to the
Municipal School of Technology. When the new building was nearing
completion, Owens College was on the point of becoming the autonomous
University of Manchester. What A. J. Balfour, opening the new municipal building in 1902, called " the greatest of this kind of municipal enterprise in the country " had sprung from a municipal consciousness which
was well aware of what was happening at Owens College, and, whilst
eagerly desiring that both ventures in higher education should proceed
in their own proper ways, was nevertheless as anxious as were the Owens
authorities to find a way of co-operation.

There had in fact been before this many occasions on which city and
university had considered their respective functions in higher education.
The city, in the 1890's, developing its higher technical instruction, wanted
to prevent overlaps with Owens College. As early as 1894, and at the
instigation of the City Council, a committee of the college and the city
had been set up to discuss the way to co-ordinate the college's and the
city's provision for technical education. In the course of negotiations,
Owens College decided to restrict its evening teaching activities to subjects not provided for " in the institutions of this city and the surrounding
district ". But that only related to evening classes. There were subjects,
already an integral part of Owens College's daytime activity, which were
also, and rightly, taught in the Technical School in the city. In 1896 an
agreement was reached; an agreed statement defined the scope of the
municipal Technical School to be " to train students in an elementary but

sound knowledge of Science and Art and to show how this knowledge may be applied to the advancement of trade and industry " ; it was also agreed that the University would recognise two years' work in the Technical School as the first year's work in the University. The situation was obviously no more than a temporary *modus vivendi*. The city was putting all its energies into the development of higher technological education, and naturally would in time desire a closer and more equitable arrangement with Owens College. In 1900, a joint committee tried to formulate the natural diversities of the Owens and the city view in a series of resolutions which disguise a relatively unwilling compromise under the terms of mutual collaboration. In 1900 the joint committee reported : " (1) that the Committee of the Manchester Municipal School of Technology recognises the supreme importance of maintaining the Owens College in its special work as a University College, teaching the arts and sciences in complete courses ; (2) that the Council of Owens College recognises the supreme importance of the Municipal School of Technology, constituted and maintained as a school of applied arts and science, to the manufacturing industries and commerce ".

The situation was clearly no more than a verbal moratorium. The city had in its service J. H. Reynolds, who was making technological education an indispensable part of any valid scheme of academic study. He recommended that the Technical School be named, as accordingly it was named, The Municipal School of Technology ; and in 1918, long after the incorporation of its more advanced work into the structure of the University, it took on the name of the College of Technology. Between 1900 and 1903, when Owens College got the charter which made it the independent University of Manchester, the city's Technical School had reached the stage when its most advanced work was unmistakably of university standard. It was work being done by men who were as qualified in knowledge and in native intelligence as were men reading for any honours degree in a university, and who were proceeding from that to a post-graduate course of academic study. The Technical School knew this, and quite rightly wished to develop such higher work. Hitherto, as we have seen, there had been negotiations between the school and the University about the definition of their respective areas. The University somewhat under-estimated both the academic quality of the school's work and the eagerness of the civic authorities to carry technology to its farthest development. The result was that in 1901 after desultory formulations of divisions in the more elementary branches of their common academic grounds, the city sought freedom to pursue its own scheme by denouncing the concordat of 1890, and, at the same time, urging the City Council to give to its own Technical School the money it had hitherto granted to Owens College. Perhaps it was a tactical move on the city's part to secure a status for technology in the independent University of Manchester which was known to be in prospect, and which received its charter in 1903. As will have emerged in our attempt to diagnose the inherent compulsions of the Owens' idea, the academic recognition of technology which the city sought was not only an indisputable consequence of the ideas implicit in Owens' purpose, but was, as Alexander was later to propound, a major enlargement in the development of the academic idea of all English universities.

In any event the University established a Faculty of Technology in 1903, that is, it prepared the official way by which it could at a later date recognise specified departments of study and research in the city's Technical School as courses qualifying for the award of a university degree. It recognised the heads of the Technical School departments which gave those courses as professors with chairs on the University Senate, and it recognised the non-professorial teachers of those subjects in the school as members of the University teaching staff. The co-operation went even more close : onto the Faculty of Technology, which was mainly comprised of those who taught university subjects in the Technical School, the University elected a number of its own university representatives of related subjects. Even more important ; all this was done in the full knowledge that the authority which finally determined the actions of the Technical School staff who had now become integral members of the University was not the University Council and Senate, but the Manchester City Council. After all, lay members of Manchester's civic community had created Owens : why should not the new development succeed ? It has indeed succeeded. The Manchester College of Technology is, if not the greatest, certainly one of the greatest institutions of its kind in Great Britain. Its success has been another of the local blood-streams by which the University has increased its vitality. In view of the intellectual outlook of the University in earlier days, Roscoe's opinion for instance, or Schuster's, it is a little ominous to find that when the inevitable recognition of Technology was being considered by the University, the discussion turned far too largely on the name which should be given to the degree which the new Faculty would award; there was an unfortunate, but sustained, effort to make it, not a degree in science, but in technology. The city's college was right, and was more true to the spirit of Owens College in insisting that it should be a degree in science, though to distinguish it from what hitherto was the normal science degree it could carry as appendix its technological origin, B.Sc.Tech. The argument about the title of the degree, settled in 1905, nevertheless indicates how the new University would have to watch where to strike the right balance between academic tradition and innovations through which alone academic life can renew itself. There still are a few responsible members of our academic community who look on technologists as out of place in an academic body. Fortunately, however, theoretic problems of that kind have not greatly affected the development of our Faculty of Technology. There has, indeed, on rare occasions, been difficulty with problems in which theory and practice were closely bound together. Certain subjects, of which engineering is the supreme example, for it is of all sciences the most palpably applied science, are taught both in the University and in The College of Technology (as after 1918 the Technical School was called). How far is it possible to delimit the strictly scientific and the strictly technological elements in this study? If it is a problem, it is insoluble. But one suspects that it is an unreal problem. At least, Roscoe and Schuster and Alexander found it unrealistic, if not unreal. It provided a situation which in practice could be resolved by compromise on both sides: men with the right spirit and the requisite common sense could work together unperturbed because at some points the scope of their interest overlapped. About 1920, on one side or the other (I do not know which, since I only became a member of Senate in 1921), there seems to have been a temporary spell of veiled hostility. It probably arose through what were thought to be invasive overlaps in Engineering and Metallurgy. As a joint committee failed to formulate a satisfactory compromise, the City gave notice that it would withdraw from participation in one particular joint city-and-university venture which had been a unique experiment to carry still further forward the idea underlying the co-operation in the Faculty of Technology. A chair of architecture had been set up by the University and the city acting together; it had been tenable both in the College of Technology and in the University. The dual control was not a success. The theoretic problem of a division in architecture between the techniques of building and the art of structural planning is almost metaphysical. In any case, Technology had a department of Building. So in 1921, the College of Technology withdrew from the joint scheme with the University for arrangements in the department of Architecture. Even to-day, no way out of that particular predicament has been found, though fortunately both College and University have found how much they gain mutually in strength by their collaboration in other spheres of academic work. One cannot help rejoicing that in Manchester University the chair of Textile Technology ranks equally with the chairs of Ancient History and of English Literature. That is a situation which admirably indicates what the " universitas " in a real university is.

The youngest of Manchester's Faculties, that of Education, established in 1914, furnishes another characteristic example of the Manchester way. From the beginning Owens College had recognised its obligation to do something for elementary school teachers : it had set up evening classes especially for them. As early as 1858, the success of these Schoolmasters' Classes in Owens College prompted a proposal from the Board of Education that Owens should be the first academic college to incorporate within it a training college. But Principal Greenwood was more conscious of risks than of opportunities in the suggestion : and so our national education system had to wait until 1890 before universities began officially to undertake responsibility for the training of teachers. In 1890, however, Manchester was one of the seven university colleges which took advantage of the new Government scheme for the institution of Day Training Colleges in close association with university colleges. The Principal of Owens College, A. W. Ward, became also in 1890 Head of the Manchester Day Training Department. This was a Department for Men ; in 1892 a parallel one for women was started. The two ran side by side, completely independent of each other, but following strictly parallel courses, until in due course they were integrated at first informally and then formally in the Department of Education. This department was the first of its kind in England ; for in 1899 Owens established a chair of Education, the first in any English university college. The professor, H. L. Withers, died after only three years' tenure. But in 1903 the new department was greatly strengthened. The University seized the opportunity offered by Michael Sadler's resignation from the service of the Board of Education and a second chair of Education was added to the department. With Findlay as Withers' successor, and Sadler

I

as an additional professor, the department set itself to take full advantage of the new orientation of academic activities made possible by the independence which Manchester secured through its Charter in 1903. Sadler had the gift of statesmanship as well as a unique knowledge of educational administration ; Findlay had an irrepressible intellectual energy and the enthusiasm which a new notion stirred in him made him a stimulating colleague and teacher. The main purpose of the Training Department which was set up in 1890 was to train elementary school teachers. But within a year or two, it was considering plans for the training of secondary school teachers as well : and in 1894, the University instituted a diploma for secondary school teachers in the theory and practice of Education. This side of its work became, of course, much more significant after Mr. Balfour's Education Act of 1901 so largely increased the provision of secondary education.

In its approach to the training of both elementary and of secondary teachers, the Manchester attitude was distinctive, and, in many ways, original. As early as 1902 the Department had realised that it needed not only real schools in which the art of teaching could be practised, just as medicine needs hospitals in which to demonstrate its practices. Like medicine, it needed something more : it needed a particular school which could be used as a kind of research laboratory. In 1902 the College opened a small primary school and kindergarten of its own : in 1905 an upper school was started, and in 1908 these were amalgamated and became the Fielden Demonstration School. Though the later history of the Fielden School was a somewhat chequered one, its institution was a sound academic venture and a definite contribution to educational exploration. It was an experiment which served its turn ; and, when the school was closed, there were other means of satisfying the needs which it at first had alone been able to satisfy.

The way from a department of Education to a Faculty of Education was an experiment and an experience in academic organisation. In 1903 the subject of Education was allocated to the Faculty of Arts, but a year later, the department was removed from Arts and was placed under the authority of a special committee of Senate. This soon became a departmental committee, comprising representatives of Science and of Arts, and reporting to both those Faculties. It was, however, becoming increasingly clear that the wide ramifications, both within the University and in the city and the county, of the department's necessary interests required a larger independence in administrative organisation. A department of education is, and must be, interested in all subjects taught in the university; it must have close and continuous contacts with every educational institution in its area, and in particular with all the elementary and secondary schools of the district. Hence the department was given a Faculty status so that it would have greater representativeness and greater freedom at one and the same time. It has made excellent use of that freedom in extending the scope of its service. In 1918 it established a department of Education for the Deaf, an academic development which has made Manchester widely known in academic America. It has recently incorporated within itself another department, that of Adult Education. It has, moreover, played its full share in the Ministry's new plan for bringing training colleges of all kinds within the ægis of a university. There is, in fact, in the University a Department of Education in the Faculty of Education: there is also a School of Education, of which our professor of education is the director, and in which our own Department is a component unit together with the recognised training colleges of our own region. It can therefore be said that, perhaps even more than those branches of university study which are called social studies, the Faculty of Education keeps the University in closer and more vital touch with the society of our province, with Training Colleges, with Technical Schools, with extra-mural organisations, with civic and with county educational authorities and all their educational associations. Moreover, beyond these systematic mechanisms for co-operating with the appropriate social units of our region, it must always be remembered that an academic department of education is, in its highest function, charged to explore the ideas on which our national educational system has been and must continue to be built. It is, in fact, the back-room laboratory of England's future as a liberal society of human beings.

The foregoing paragraphs have noted the proliferation of the University's academic activities in its larger units of organisation. But, of course, the progress of a university depends on its getting the right individuals as its members of staff. In particular, it depends on the quality of scholarship it recruits to its professorial body. Between 1880 and 1890, Schuster, Stirling, Lamb and Dixon became professors. Between 1890 and 1904, Tout, Alexander, Perkin, Hickson, Weiss and Peake came to us. Between 1900 and 1914 Manchester was singularly fortunate in adding to its Senate men who were, like those just named, to give the University international reputation in their own fields of scholarship and research. Of others who became professors in Manchester between 1900 and 1914 there were Conway, Herford, Moulton, Tait, Unwin, Findlay, Chapman, Rutherford, Petavel, Lang, Holland and Elliot Smith; and each of these names is permanently recorded in the history of scholarship. By this time, too, the characteristics which were distinctive of the Manchester way of the academic life were widely recognised, and those who came on to its staff came with broad sympathy for the Tout-Alexander concept of its function as a university. It was a doctrine, too, which was shared not only by the teaching and administrative staff of the University : essential articles of it were preached by its successive Chancellors from 1904 to the present day.

John Morley, later Lord Morley, accepting the Chancellorship in 1908, said that he prized it " for its local association with the great and powerful county in which I happily chance to have been born ". Himself a scholar, a humanist, and a bookman, on his visits to Manchester he used to remind students of the value of the pursuit of knowledge not only as a mental discipline, but as a way in which the University exercises a great and wholesome influence on the outside world, where academic habits of weighing the meaning of words, of considering all sides of a question, could check " the frightful impulse to rush to angry sides " on important and delicate public questions. He was a fine embodiment of the North-Country belief in plain living, high thinking, and hard work. In the life intellectual, he sought constant communion with the best in thought and in art : but one of his strongest convictions was that such communion was barren unless fructified by active participation in the world's business and affairs.

Even more energetically did Lord Morley's successor, Lord Crawford, expound the same Manchester academic gospel. He used to say, in the deliberative, slow, majestic tone which admirably became his manner and his appearance, that he was publicly known as the premier Scots baron, whereas in reality, he was a Lancashire coal merchant. When he was installed as Chancellor in 1923, he spoke of his deep affection for and keen interest in the life of our throbbing Lancashire community, and told how excited he was to contemplate the wide extent to which the university might contribute to the enrichment of its province. It was not only our privilege, but our duty, he said, to analyse the special needs of our district, to embrace and comprehend them all, and thus to respond to all the varied and complex requirements of our county. That we

LORD SIMON OF WYTHENSHAWE, CHAIRMAN OF COUNCIL 1941–

could do, and must insist on doing, without relaxing one jot the highest
academic standards of the intellectual life.   Throughout his Chancellorship, Lord Crawford's consistent effort was to strengthen the ties between
the University and the life of our region.   By the unobtrusive grace
with which he received regional dignitaries, mayors and other representatives of North-Country towns, he inspired in them a feeling of fellowship
in a high social endeavour.   He made them realise that the well-being of
all of us depended in a literal, even a material sense, on the encouragement
of cultural education and of scientific discovery.   He persuaded them that
the universities, even in those of their activities traditionally followed in
Faculties of Arts, were in fact pursuing researches inspired by the will
" to lead learning forward to great ends and to constructive ideals ".
Lord Crawford, as Chancellor, was a magnificent embodiment of the
Roscoe-Ward-Schuster-Tout-Alexander ideal of a university and of the
rôle which it could play in social and public life.   One vivid memory
of him may not here be out of place.   He lived near his coalpits at Haigh
Hall, Wigan.   He had there his magnificent Bibliotheca Lindesiana, the
library accumulated by four centuries of his Lindsay stock.   He was
also a trustee of Manchester's John Rylands Library : and he arranged
an exhibition of the riches of his own library at Haigh Hall for the delecta-
tion of the Governors of the John Rylands.   At his own suggestion,
various Manchester professors were invited along with those who were
governors of the John Rylands Library.   I asked Professor Daniels to
join us.   Daniels was pure Lancashire.   He had worked in a pit in his
youth, and afterwards as an electrician.   Through extra-mural classes,
followed by Ruskin College, he had continued his education.   At the
instigation of Sydney Chapman, he returned to study in Manchester
University, and in due course, Chapman appointed him to the Economics
staff; in 1921 he was made professor.   He in himself was an irrefutable
justification of the idea of Redbrick universities.   On the trip to Haigh
Hall we were much together.   On leaving, our omnibus was drawn up
outside the front door of the Hall, and, as the engine started, Lord and
Lady Crawford waved us an informal farewell.   Daniels, who was an
ardent democrat, a Liberal with an intense Radical faith, turned to me and
said as he looked at Lord and Lady Crawford, " You know, it's worth
five centuries of breeding to breed two like those."

    Of Lord Crawford's successor as Chancellor, Lord Woolton, it only
needs to be said that he is Manchester-minded, Manchester-trained, and

intuitively conscious of Manchester University's function in the academic world. And therefore, in the short space of five years since his installation, he has made it his business, to an extent beyond that of any other of our Chancellors, to interest himself personally in every sphere of our activities. He does not merely appear on big ceremonial occasions. He has made himself familiar with the day to day life of the institution. He is known to the students, visits the Halls of Residence and the University Settlement. In this way he is not only making University history, he is making a contribution to our general well-being which is becoming more and more widely realised.

Our argument, however, is becoming more and more difficult to contain within the limits of its purpose, which is to trace the evolution of the Owens' idea into the University of Manchester. During the time when the Tout-Alexander version of it was being firmly established, Sir Alfred Hopkinson was Vice-Chancellor of the University. He had succeeded Ward as Principal of Owens College in 1898, had put all his legal acumen and local patriotism into leading the Manchester campaign for independence, and continuously gave full sympathy and authoritative support to the major articles of the Tout-Alexander academic faith. When he retired in 1913, in a letter to Lord Morley, explaining his motive for resigning, he added an illuminating summary of the University's achievements during his Vice-Chancellorship :

" I believe that there is a period in the history of an institution full of life, as our University is, when a change is desirable, and when a new administrative Head may bring in fresh vigour and exercise a stronger influence than one who has held the office so long as I have. It was impossible to take this step when such vital matters were pending as the position of the University with regard to Government grants and its relation to the Board of Education and the Treasury in dealing with such grants. These questions affected not only the University of Manchester, but also the whole future position of Universities aided by the State. Most of them are now settled in a manner which is generally satisfactory, and, in the course of the next three months, the settlement of the few matters that remain will be completed. Our relations with the City, County, and other Local Authorities, and also with the Educational Institutions in the district, are of a most friendly character. The arrangement with the School of Technology is working satisfactorily. The reconstitution of the University, when new Universities were created in

Liverpool and Leeds, is fully carried out, and the consequent arrangements that have been made enable us to deal with many important subjects in co-operation with these Universities. New buildings have been erected since 1900 at a cost of about £190,000 (exclusive of the Whitworth Hall, for which Mr. Christie had provided), and this amount has, except a few hundred pounds, been paid. During the same period the endowments producing income have increased, the teaching staff has been greatly enlarged, and fresh subjects included in the work of the University, but no debts have been accumulated, and the annual expenditure for several years has not exceeded the income. The special problems that presented themselves at the time of my appointment and on the re-organisation of the University have now been dealt with, and the moment accordingly seems opportune for putting into new hands the new developments or work which the University will undertake."

When Sir Alfred Hopkinson resigned in 1913, Professor Weiss was persuaded to act as Vice-Chancellor until a long-term appointment could be made. He acted for two years, and at the end of the first of them, 1914, came the war. In 1915 Sir Henry Miers became Vice-Chancellor.

Sir Henry had had long experience of academic administration in London University. Perhaps, too, the fact that he was a direct descendant of Francis Place, the tailor Radical of the early nineteenth century, was a special recommendation to Manchester men, although Sir Henry, they knew, had been educated at Eton and at Oxford, and was a Fellow of Eton College. Inevitably, his first three years in Manchester were occupied with temporary adaptations to suit from week to week the changing circumstances of war-time. Moreover, in the University itself, academic progress was properly secondary to the problem of discovering how the University could contribute towards the paramount need, the securing of our national survival. Experienced administrator as he was, he was greatly handicapped by inevitable situations : the war years did not give him opportunity to see the University's normal and characteristic way of life, an academic life vastly different from that either in London or in Oxford. Moreover, he was himself vividly aware that for a Southerner, and a Londoner especially, to acclimatise himself physically, civically and humanly to Manchester and its people is a formidable task. He was Vice-Chancellor from 1915 to 1926. Three years after he resigned, he wrote reminiscently of " Some Characteristics of Manchester Men ". One sees that he never really saw through the " sordid background of materialism " against which Manchester men, as he said, stand in high relief. Manchester itself was drab : had it a drab mind ? " You have in Manchester a population that may require stirring to free itself from the sordid inheritance of the too rapid industrial growth of the city in the nineteenth century." It is clear that Sir Henry was always strongly conscious of " the smoke, the noise, the rain, and the squalor that so often pervade the district ". Even when he had been Vice-Chancellor for eight years, and it was his duty to write an address to Lord Crawford, just chosen as our new Chancellor, he wrote : " May your advent to Manchester, my Lord, be an inspiration to those who desire to redeem this city from the unseemly conditions of its industrial life, and to restore, as far as may be, its ancient heritage of beauty." Lord Crawford had, indeed, a much deeper intuitive sense of the place, and of the danger of confusing appearance and reality in appreciating the spirit of Manchester and the purpose of Manchester University. Sir Henry would have found incomprehensible, and perhaps set down as mere literary sentiment, the view of Manchester expressed by a leader-writer in the *Manchester Guardian* in 1930, on the occasion of the University's fiftieth anniversary :

    " The civic universities are civic in no narrowing or parochial sense. They draw a large part of their direct support from their respective cities, and they aim to express their gratitude by making themselves an organic member of the city life through their devotion to their special office of diffusing knowledge and creating fresh knowledge. But though local in their origin they are national in their outlook. Like trees, they draw their sustenance from their own soil, but aspire into and spread their branches in the common atmosphere. And the day has long gone by when it could be doubted if a great industrial centre like Manchester were the suitable or the best place for a University. Such doubters forgot the active life of Florence, where Galileo lived and Leonardo and Michael Angelo. Where the pulse of life is highest, in the great congregations of men, and men's energies in manufacture and trade are at their highest strain, there also the other energies have their likeliest play. Science and the arts are the flowering, and, in one sense of that vague word, the romance of life. True romance is not, however, remote from the daily life : it is rooted in it. It is a dull eye which cannot penetrate through the dirt and fog of Manchester to its underlying poetry. Indeed Lancashire may claim to be, even in the face of Yorkshire, the most romantic of English counties and yet a vast field of industrial work."

However, the war years and the immediately post-war ones required mainly the kind of administrative control which is skilled in adjustments to new, and, as it turned out, unsuspectedly new, circumstances. Sir Henry Miers's national reputation inevitably meant that he was called in to advise on more general organisations than that of one university. He had, therefore, very frequently to spend more time in London than in Manchester. Indeed, when his term of office expired and leave was officially taken of him at a university dinner, the proposer of the toast, speaking in commendation and not in criticism of Sir Henry, said that one outstanding feature of his service to Manchester had been his accessibility to all members of the staff: he could be found invariably on two or three days a week in the dining-car of the Euston–Manchester railway train.

His experience was very valuable in coping with post-war problems. In the major one, the unexpected doubling of student-numbers, it was a stroke of high fortune that his skill in organising a general trend could be translated into the appropriate Manchester modification of it by Fiddes, who was acting, and in many ways, as effective deputy Vice-Chancellor. It would therefore be neither unkind nor unfair to say of Sir Henry's tenure of office, that in that period the idea of Manchester University took on no new direction, it followed its inherent and native development. Sir Henry did, however, help greatly with Fiddes as co-adjutator in tidying up the mechanisms by which the main features of the Owens' idea were sustained.

The importance of this consolidation is well illustrated by a situation which provided one of the many post-war problems. No one had foreseen the rate at which the demand for university education would rise. A new Arts Building had been planned just before the European war. The contract for it was signed a day or two before war broke out in August, 1914. It was planned to satisfy a thirty- to fifty-year normal expansion. When it was first occupied in 1919, it was so overcrowded that straightway one of the larger Arts departments had to be evicted. The victim was the English department, whose chief, Professor Herford, had as great an international reputation in scholarship as any of his Arts colleagues, except perhaps Tout, but who was a mere babe in political strategy and tactics. He was exiled, with his department, to Lime House. The compulsory removal, however, unexpectedly brought with it the kind of rewards which innocence often enjoys in spite of the schemes of the politicians. In the first place, moving into Lime House, the department which was given to the study of the æsthetic phenomenon known as literature, found itself housed in a building previously occupied by a well-known and well-respected organiser and trainer of successive bands of terpsichorian artists collectively known eponymously as the Tiller Girls. Moreover, within a very short time, Lime House, an outer-Hebridean territory of the main Arts island, became geographically more and more the pivotal centre of Arts activities. A new Arts Library was built on that side of Lime House which was further away from the New Arts Building. More recently still, remoter property, the adapted German Church (in our plan p. 172 labelled Library Extension), and the new Arts overflow building (in the plan, Arts Extension), lie on that side of Lime House which is still farther away from the Arts Building. In an Arts Faculty, the core, the formative and nuclear centre is the Library. Lime House is on its doorstep.

If, then, during Sir Henry's tenure, there had been no distinctively Mancunian expansions of our academic activity, if the policy was rather to corroborate activities already incorporated in the University rather than to experiment with projects in peripheral fields of academic study, if very few new chairs except such as that of Russian (1919), that of Italian (1920), and the second chair of Economics (1921), which were established as the immediate political outcome of the war, at least one of these consequential and politically prompted pieces of organisation is of special importance. As has already been seen, the degree of Ph.D. was instituted. Its establishment naturally led to more deliberate organisation of postgraduate work; and in particular, it offered to Tout the opportunity to fulfil his academic ideal by building up a bigger and bigger post-graduate school of historical research.

In 1924, just before he retired from the vice-chancellorship, Sir Henry must have read with pleasure a tribute to the achievements of the University of Manchester publicly expressed by the Vice-Chancellor of Birmingham University, Sir Charles Grant Robertson, in a letter to the press :

" The historian of fifty years hence will mark the foundation of Owens College as the commencement of a great educational movement which has resulted to-day in the existence of seven provincial universities, of four university colleges, and of the University of Wales with its four constituent colleges. Owens College provided both the model and the inspiration to other important and developing industrial centres. It inspired, to take one example, the beneficent generosity of Sir Josiah Mason at Birmingham : and no one who has read Huxley's famous address on the opening of Mason's College in 1879 but will realise what it owes to those who founded Owens College five-and-twenty years earlier.

" The foundation and endowment of a college, however, are only the beginning. The vital and decisive forces are the ideals, policy, and personality of those who are called upon to nurse the infant from the cradle to maturity. It would be as invidious as it is wholly unnecessary, particularly for anyone who is not Manchester born and bred, to attempt to allocate the respective shares of Sir A. W. Ward and of that small but brilliant band of colleagues who made Owens College in fullness of time the inevitable parent of the University of Manchester. What the college and then the University has been, and still more will be, in the life of Lancashire and of Great Britain can be safely left to those immediately concerned to decide. What is far more important is to put, briefly, on record the immense influence their work at Manchester had on the rest of England, and how their ideals, their faith, their methods, and their work have profoundly affected the development of higher education and secured, precept upon precept, line upon line, the deepening national conviction that a higher liberal education through science and the humanistic subjects, linked together, could be secured in the capitals of the great industrial provinces of England and Wales. No less important was the proof that the colleges and then the nascent universities could become centres of learning and research, and that the efficiency of their purely educational work was dependent on the indissoluble marriage between teaching and post-graduate investigation. How this has in turn revolutionised the whole conception of secondary education and has, also, influenced the ancient universities of Oxford and Cambridge is a story, the truth and detail of which it is desirable we should not forget."

The more we come down to our own day, the more invidious becomes the task of naming the new-comers who signally enlarged or added new impetus to the Manchester academic idea. But no one can feel underrated if the following recruitments to professorial chairs during Sir Henry Miers's vice-chancellorship are cited as especially noteworthy in our academic life : Powicke, Stopford, Bragg, Daniels, Robinson and Stocks : and of the special way in which the Manchester academic mission is intuitively comprehended by academic "foreigners", be they from Oxford or Cambridge. Stocks is an outstanding example. Son of the parsonage, Rugby for school, Oxford for university, and a long spell as Oxford don and college Fellow, he showed himself when he came to us to be keenly interested in all progressive enterprises and especially in all branches of learning which seek to explore the relationship of human beings to each other in society. He strongly supported the social studies, as formal academic disciplines, such as sociology, public administration, and so forth. Still more, he insisted that it was a national duty obligatory on university members, in their social capacity, to contribute to such educational or civic projects as popular adult education or housing estates or university settlements or community organisations. Incidentally, Stocks was an international hockey player, an aggressive batsman, and a golfer who would have been even nearer to scratch if he could have been persuaded that a cricket swing is not the best golf swing. And human details such as these are not irrelevant to the tracing of the Manchester idea : for in every case, it is the humanity or the humaneness of its exponents, even more than their technical expertise, which has made them productive bearers of the Manchesterness of Manchester University. One hears much, perhaps too much, of what Manchester University suffers through not being a residential university. But as far as its staff is concerned, it possesses one institution, Staff House, established in 1939, which had then no real parallel in any of the modern universities, and which can fulfil in some respects, by its wider representativeness, a function exceeding that of an Oxford or Cambridge common-room. Day after day hundreds of the teaching and administrative staff foregather inside it, and conversation runs at every human level over all conceivable topics of human interest. It is here more than elsewhere that the Manchester climate of university opinion fashions itself.

After Sir Henry Miers, our Vice-Chancellor was Sir Walter Moberly, who ruled, or rather in the more appropriate Manchester idiom, who held office from 1926 to 1934. During this period, the University could once more resume its normal organic line of growth without interruption by adventitious circumstance. The student population, 1,655 in 1913/14, 2,775 in 1919/20, seemed to be settling at a normal figure just reaching towards 3,000. Sir Walter, knowing Oxford as undergraduate and as College Fellow, had also known academic teaching life in Birmingham University for a short while, and had been Principal of

Exeter University College. For anyone who had the privilege of working in Manchester during Sir Walter's vice-chancellorship, it is impossible not to realise to what a wide extent his influence here was incontestably of high, and indeed of unique, value. It is also almost impossible not to venture to be critical of some implications of his academic ideals and to find them less valid guides for Manchester's progress, not because their inherent doctrine is in itself fallacious but because it moves through modes not native to the Manchester character.

Essentially the spirit of his endeavour was in the straight and fundamental direction of the Manchester idea : namely, a passionate conviction that a university's function is to render its unique service to the highest interests of humanity. He had a devout faith, and it animated all his actions, that the universities ought to be primary instruments in opening a higher spiritual life both to individuals and, through them, to the community at large. He was eager to impress upon the whole University its corporate responsibility to society. As far as its formal academic activities were concerned, he was especially concerned to remind the Faculty of Arts of its traditional humanising objectives, of its rôle in the making and the preserving of a civilised and civilising culture. He urged it not to fail in this essential service by a too easy assumption that the ways and the values of the physical sciences were necessarily the right criteria for the disciplines of the humanities. He implored the Faculty of Arts above all not to succumb to the mere weight of its own erudition. On the other side of his province as Vice-Chancellor, that which is not concerned with the trends of university teaching, but is occupied with the students' social sense and the realisation by them of their integral partnership in the fellowship, and therefore in the responsibilities and the duties, of the University, he was eager to foster all those extra-tutorial and extra-classroom organisations which aim at strengthening those elements in character through which the student becomes conscious of and fulfils his obligations to his fellow-men.

Hence, one who has spent his life in Manchester University may be permitted to say that although there appear to be considerable differences in formulation between Sir Walter's ideal university and the historic Manchester idea of a university, there is a close similarity in the spirit which animates both. It is only when the spirit seeks to formulate itself in creed that the dissidence appears. One may, for instance, have a passionate belief that only when a university perpetually reminds itself that its healthiest intellectual atmosphere is that of " crisis " will it fulfil its specific function, namely its exercise of the liberty of thought in pursuit of elusive truth in those vast territories of the unknown from which each generation may wrest its little addition to the cumulative stock of what can be truly called the known. For, academically, a crisis is only a recognition that judgments are to be made, that there are problems which are to be explored, and answers to them sought. Intellectually, " crisis " is the supreme motive of enquiry, which, in its turn, is the specific temper of the university mind. It is, at all events, the intellectual temper which prompted the progress of Manchester University. However, even one who believes in that kind of a mental atmosphere as the right one for a university would have recognised that, for nine-tenths of the way, he would have adopted the same procedure and approved the same policies as those Sir Walter favoured in Manchester. He would at the same time have recognised how much more salutary for the traditionally humane studies was Sir Walter's doctrine compared with that in which learning is desiccated into mere erudition.

Sir Walter Moberly resigned in 1934 in response to an invitation to become the first full-time chairman of the University Grants Committee, a high tribute to the esteem he had earned as a wise academic administrator. He was succeeded in the vice-chancellorship by Professor, now Sir John, Stopford. Steeped from youth in the Manchester tradition, knowing, too, the life of Manchester University both as student and as teacher in it, sharing instinctively in a deep sense of the University's obligation to serve mankind, he has translated Moberly's ideal into the academic idiom and into the native habit of Manchester University. Fortunately he had five clear years before the outbreak of the world war. In those early years he laid out the direction and the means to immediate development, and was prepared with plans and mechanisms for its achievement. But the war came. It fell to him to guide the University through its biggest trial. The problems arising during the war were sufficiently exacting for any Vice-Chancellor, and more so, for one whose genius for administration soon found itself burdened with more and more national, as distinct from Manchester, academic problems. Within the University, almost every one of its customary activities was re-orientated : temporarily it was bending all its efforts to an essentially public and non-academic emergency. With the coming of peace, the problems of administration stretched almost to breaking-point. Student numbers jumped from 2,774 in 1938/39, to

4,898 in 1946/47, 5,570 in 1947/48, and nearly 6,000 in 1948/49. The really pressing problem of policy was to find how far such inflation was compatible not only with Manchester's, but with the traditional English notion, of what is implied by a University education. Moreover, the University was called upon by the Government to extend its academic operations into fields hitherto but sparsely provided for, if not completely neglected. By Government instigation and by Government support, three wider areas of academic study and research were incorporated in the Manchester scope. In 1931 Alexander, as has been recorded in these pages, named the integration of Technology within the University's intellectual orbit as the distinctive hall-mark of the Manchester way in the realisation of a new and vital conception of a university. Now in 1950, it could be as safely asserted that, at least with three of the new territories added to its intellectual continent, an even more decisive step has been taken in the natural progress of the Manchester academic idea. The three lie within the provinces of Education, Medicine, and the Social Sciences, and of these, especially, in Medicine and the Social Sciences. The wide extension of the scope of our medical studies, marked by the creation of new professorships in the Faculty of Medicine (ten have been established since 1938) reminds us that Manchester has always had a sense that medicine was first of the Social Sciences and that, in effect, it could be, to the twentieth century, what the classical humanities were to the sixteenth. By the Clapham Committee's recommendation, our chairs in the Social Sciences, in the limited sense now current, have been increased threefold ; and the Social Sciences are the indispensable academic technologies of the humanities, the means by which the humanities can be kept in touch with the needs of human beings and of real human life, if only the Social Sciences will not succumb to their own specific technique, that is, if they will not allow statistics to become a devitalising force like the erudition which turns humane learning into pedantry. Social Science, like the humanities, must preserve its essentially moral core. Jubilation may perhaps be somewhat less general about our academic accretions through the Scarbrough report. They seem at Manchester to throw the major stress in academic arts pursuits on the exploration of antiquity. Of course, the prosecution, with the full rigour of real academic method, of any field of knowledge is, in its own rights, a proper university activity. But there are priorities in values when this or the other field is chosen from the immense number still to be systematically adopted : care must be taken to see that the faculty, which, with the Renaissance exaltation of the Greek and Roman classics, became the focus of those studies which were called humane because of their direct bearing on real and contemporary human problems, does not acquire a preference for subjects which by their remoteness in time have become the merely " academic ". The Arts Faculty loses its character if it reverts to what medicine grew out of when it realised that the study of corpses was only a preliminary to its own real field of operation, and to where zoologists were before they passed from museum specimens to the living objects in their aquaria and vivaria. An Arts Faculty must never be a mere museum : for it, archæology, in its limited and in its most extended senses, the study of the past, whether in linguistics, in institutions, or in literature, is only one, and that, too, only the preliminary groundwork from which its real purpose can be projected. The fifteenth and sixteenth centuries, rediscovering the humanities of the classical world, had found a source of new life for the universities. Oxford and Cambridge in those years were making scholarship an active instrument in the furtherance of civilisation. From the same classical source, moreover, they were implicitly and explicitly reminded of the dangers inherent in scholarship, reminded especially by Plutarch, and reminded in a volume of Plutarch put into cogent Elizabethan English by Philemon Holland. There was one point on which Plutarch concurred with his Stoic opponent, Chrysippus : it was on the liability of the " scholastical life " to show little ostensible difference from " the life of voluptuous persons ". Plutarch agrees with Chrysippus that " they who thinke this scholastical and idle life of students even from the beginning is most of all beseeming and agreeable to philosophers, in my conceit, seeme much deceived, weening as they do that they are to philosophize for their pastime or recreation, and so to draw out in length the whole course of their life at their booke in their studies, which is as much to say in plaine tearmes, as to live at ease and in pleasure ". For himself, Plutarch roundly accuses most scholastics of neglecting their duties, " only to this end that they might lead their lives more sweetly at their pleasure, studying and disputing with ease, *and letting out their girdle slacke as they list themselves* ". But despite our recently increased commitments to a remoter past, Manchester is by its very location saved from too large inroads of the academic anæmia which Plutarch diagnoses. At any rate, though the Scarbrough Report has extended our academic stretch backwards, we have, of our own pure motion, taken a lead in establishing a chair of American Studies, set up in

LORD WOOLTON, Chancellor of the University, 1944–

1948, with a title in which American means, not Aztec nor red-skin, but of and belonging to the United States of America.

Still, in Manchester it has usually happened that whatever its teachers have professed, whether a seemingly unpromising or an obviously exciting subject, their way of pursuing it has given it vitality. One hopes and believes that this will go on happening. In the meantime, and at the moment, surveying the outstanding developments of recent years in Medicine and in the Social Sciences (and the widening of our Faculty of Law is part of this), there can be no hesitation in recognising them as an integral development of the organic idea of Manchester University. One realises also how much the medical side of that development is primarily Sir John Stopford's contribution, not only to his university, but to the enlarging of the country's idea of a university. One rejoices, too, that in this period of rapid expansion, still in 1950 in full process, we have our Vice-Chancellor to maintain the balance of Manchester's academic values in a period of artificially or at least extraneously motivated academic expansion, expansion in numbers of students, of subjects and of teachers.

Perhaps the most obvious gap in the scope of our academic structure is the absence of proper provision for the study and encouragement of the Fine Arts. We have of course a Faculty of Music : but we have no chair of Music. Moreover, we have tended to leave the graphic and plastic arts very inadequately represented. As early as 1872 Senate recommended the establishment of a chair in the Fine Arts, with dreams of a Manchester Slade School. Nothing came of the plan. In 1913 there was a proposal to establish courses for teachers of art, and to award a degree in the subject. Senate concurred in the notion of a degree if its institution was recognised by the setting up of a full professorship of the Fine Arts : it recommended a conference between the City Education Committee, the Municipal School of Art and the University. Hearing of this the (Manchester) Royal Institution offered a subsidy to initiate a chair, if the University would appoint a particular person to it. But Senate was unwilling to do this, and the whole scheme was pushed into the background by the outbreak of the European War. In 1922 there was another effort by the Faculty of Arts to press on Senate and Council the need for adequate representations of an academic discipline in the Fine Arts ; they urged a chair and an Honours School more or less on the lines of the Honours School of Architecture. But again nothing substantial was done : and the Fine Arts fell to casual lectures, extra-mural courses and

K

those departments in which archæology was thought of in terms of statues and vases rather than of hypercausts and drains. The University has, however, for some years now had a lecturer in the History of Art. In a place like Manchester, however, with its public galleries and with its School of Art, there should be full academic cognisance of the Fine Arts as a necessary element in a university. If city and university would come together, as they did with technology, a Faculty of Fine Arts could be set up and with the pooling of our joint resources and our joint experience, the Fine Arts could be integrated with the province's organisation of higher education. Such co-operation would be completely in the spirit of the Owens Trust. It would be in the Manchester tradition. It would be the consummation of the idea of our university.

In the meantime, *salva sit universitas nostra Mancuniensis.   Amen.*

APPENDICES

NOTE

THE theme of this volume has been to trace what, perhaps somewhat presumptuously, has been thought of as the spirit of Manchester University. But such a spirit, like all others, lives only in and by its corporeal and material incarnation. The following appendices provide information about the material framework and substance within and through which the Manchester spirit realised itself. They present facts about the personnel and the means; officers, teaching staff, student numbers (and a special appendix on what from the point of view of numbers was of vital importance, the opening of the university to women students), buildings, financial resources, benefactions, public grants and so on. But chief of all appendices which measure the growth of a university ought to be a list of the publications of its staff and of its students down the hundred years. The compilation of such a bibliography, however, is beyond our present scope. To judge from the ninety-page list in Hartog, which is truncated and moreover runs only to 1900, and from the published bibliographies of Reynolds, Schuster, Ward and Tout, the provision of such a record would increase twenty-fold the size of the present volume: and in the compilation of it there would be necessary a discrimination which could only be exercised by persons well versed in the particular branches of learning represented by each item in the list. But a Short Title Catalogue of books and articles published by Manchester staff and Manchester students would be a superb ocular demonstration of the place of Manchester in the academic polity of Great Britain. Some day some such list will be drawn up.

APPENDIX I

CHRONOLOGICAL

1846. 29th July. Death of John Owens (b. 1790).

1851. 12th March. Owens College, founded by the will of John Owens and by him placed under the control of private trustees, opened in Quay Street, Deansgate, Manchester.

1870. *The Owens Extension College Act* brought into legal being The Owens Extension College, financed by funds raised for the purpose, and competent to undertake activities not provided for by the terms of the Owens Trust. The Extension College was not a private trust; it had a more normal form of constitution and of public trusteeship. Both its staff and its governors were common to it and to Owens College.

1871. *The Owens College Act* amalgamated the two colleges and their resources as The Owens College, which began its new form of existence on 1st September 1871.

1873. The Owens College left Quay Street for its new (and present) site in the Oxford Road.

1880. 20th April. The Victoria University received its charter, The Owens College becoming its first, and for a time, its only constituent college.

1883. A supplemental charter gave The Victoria University the power to grant degrees in medicine.

1884. 5th November. University College, Liverpool, became a constituent college of the University.

1887. 3rd November. Yorkshire College, Leeds, became a constituent college of the University.

1903. 15th July. By charter the independent Victoria University of Manchester came into being and existed side by side with The Owens College, the staff of which was also the University staff.

1904. 24th June. *The Victoria University of Manchester Act* incorporated The Owens College with the new Victoria University of Manchester.

APPENDIX II

OFFICERS OF THE COLLEGE AND UNIVERSITY

A. OWENS COLLEGE BEFORE THE VICTORIA UNIVERSITY OF MANCHESTER (1903)

Chairman of Owens' Trustees :
1845. George Faulkner, died 1862.
1862. William Neild, died 1864.
1864. Alfred Neild who under the new constitution of 1870/71 became Treasurer and Chairman of the College Council.

President of the College (an office created by the 1870/71 constitution) :
1871. William Cavendish, seventh Duke of Devonshire, died 1891.
1891. Spencer Compton Cavendish, eighth Duke of Devonshire, who held the office until it lapsed in 1904 when The Owens College was amalgamated with The Victoria University of Manchester.

Treasurer of the College and Chairman of the Council :
1871. Alfred Neild, resigned 1887.
1887. Joseph Thompson, who in 1904, when the College Council lapsed, continued as Treasurer to the University.

Principals of the College :
1851. A. J. Scott, resigned 1857.
1857. J. G. Greenwood, resigned 1889.
1889. Adolphus W. Ward, resigned 1897.
1898. Alfred Hopkinson, until 1904 when he continued in office as Vice-Chancellor of the Victoria University of Manchester.

Registrar :
1851. J. P. Ashton (whose title was secretary to the Trustees).
1853. J. Holme Nicholson (whose title was clerk and librarian, a title changed in 1867 to that of Registrar), resigned 1884.
1884. H. W. Holder, resigned 1895 to become Bursar.
1895. Sydney Chaffers, to 1904 when he became Bursar.

Librarian :

    1851. George Mattinson, resigned 1853.

    1853. J. Holme Nicholson, resigned 1871.

    1871. H. C. Oats, resigned 1871.

    1871. J. Taylor Kay, resigned 1894.

    1895. J. H. Clarke, died 1895.

    1895. W. E. Rhodes, resigned 1903.

    1903. C. W. E. Leigh, acting-librarian until 1905 when he became librarian to the University.

Secretary to the University Extension Committee :

    1895 to 1903. P. J. (later Sir Philip) Hartog.

Chairman of Convocation :

    1898. Arthur Smithells.

    1899 to 1901. Horace (later Sir Horace) Lamb.

    1901 to 1905. Arthur H. Worthington.

B. Offices Created by the Formation of the (Federal) Victoria University (1880)

Visitor :

    1880. Her Majesty, Queen Victoria.

    1901. His Majesty, King Edward VII.

Chancellor :

    1880. William Cavendish, seventh Duke of Devonshire, died 1891.

    1891. John Poyntz, fifth Earl Spencer, who held office until 1907.

Vice-Chancellor :

    1880. J. G. Greenwood, term of office expired 1887.

    1887. Adolphus W. Ward, term of office expired 1891.

    1891. Gerald H. Rendall (University College, Liverpool), term of office expired 1895.

    1895. Adolphus W. Ward, resigned 1897.

    1897. Nathan Bodington (Yorkshire College), term of office expired 1901.

    1901. Alfred Hopkinson, who on the break-up of the federal university, continued as the Vice-Chancellor of the Victoria University of Manchester.

C. Officers of the Victoria University of Manchester, 1903 onwards

Visitor :

    1903. His Majesty, King Edward VII.

    1910. His Majesty, King George V.

1936. His Majesty, King Edward VIII.
1936. His Majesty, King George VI.

Chancellor :

1903. John Poyntz, fifth Earl Spencer, continued until 1907 in the office which he had held in the federal university.
1907. Spencer Compton Cavendish, eighth Duke of Devonshire (died 1908).
1908. John, Viscount Morley of Blackburn, resigned 1923.
1923. David Alexander Edward Lindsay, twenty-seventh Earl of Crawford and tenth earl of Balcarres (died 1940).
1944–   Frederick James Marquis, first Baron Woolton.

Vice-Chancellor :

1903. Sir Alfred Hopkinson, resigned 1913.
1913. Frederick Ernest Weiss, term of office expired 1915.
1915. Sir Henry Alexander Miers, term of office expired 1926.
1926. Sir Walter Hamilton Moberly, resigned 1934.
1934. Sir John S. B. Stopford.

Chairman of Council :

1904–1924. Sir Frank Forbes Adam.
1924–1934. Arthur Henry Worthington.
1934–1941. Sir Christopher T. Needham.
1941–   Sir Ernest D. Simon (later Lord Simon of Wythenshawe).

Treasurer :

1904–1908. Joseph Thompson.
1908–1913. Edward John Broadfield.
1913–1915. Hermann Woolley.
1915–1921. Alfred Ernest Steinthal.
1921–1924. Sir Christopher Needham.
1924–1932. Ernest Alfred Knight.
1932–1941. Sir Ernest D. Simon.
1941–   Sir William Clare Lees.

Registrar :

1904–1920. Edward Fiddes.
1920–1945. Norman Smith.
1945–   W. Mansfield Cooper.
1951–   (Joint Registrar) Vincent Knowles.

Bursar :

1904–1928. Sydney Chaffers.
1928–1950. G. W. Kaye.
1950–   R. A. Rainford.

Librarian :
1905–1936.   C. W. E. Leigh.
1936–   Moses Tyson.

University Extension Committee ; Secretary :
1904–1905.   W. G. S. Adams (later Warden of All Souls College, Oxford).
1905–1907.   Sydney (later Sir) P. P. Waterlow.
1908–1920.   H. P. Turner, who continued the work, first as External Registrar (1920–1926) and then as Director of Extra-Mural Studies (1926–1937).
1937–   (Director of Extra-Mural Studies) R. D. Waller (later Professor of Adult Education).

Secretary to the University Press :
1912–1949.   H. M. McKechnie.
1949–   T. L. Jones.

Chairman of Convocation :
1905–1908.   Alfred Ernest Steinthal.
1908–1911.   Dr. Robert Briggs Wild.
1911–1914.   Sir Christopher Needham.
1914–1922.   Alfred Haworth.
1922–1925.   Mrs. M. Tout.
1925.   Miss E. Needham.
1926.   Mr. A. E. G. Chorlton.
1927.   Dr. H. V. White.
1928.   His Honour Judge F. E. Bradley.
1929.   Rev. Dr. H. McLachlan.
1930.   Prof. F. E. Tylecote.
1931.   Dr. C. P. Lapage.
1932.   Mr. L. F. Behrens.
1933.   Rev. T. M. Gribbin.
1934.   Mrs. Mary E. Hogg.
1935.   Dr. T. A. Goodfellow.
1936.   Mr. David Cardwell.
1937.   Dr. C. E. Sykes.
1938.   Mr. R. H. Clayton.
1939.   Sir Frederick Marquis (created Lord Woolton during his tenure of office).
1940.   Lord Woolton.
1941–1945.   Mr. John Coatman.
1946–1948.   Dr. G. N. Burkhardt.
1949–1950.   Dr. Erna Reiss.

APPENDIX III

FINANCIAL RESOURCES OF THE UNIVERSITY

THE list of benefactions in the A section of this appendix was compiled by R. A. Rainford, Bursar. The Income Account, section B of this appendix, is taken, as far as the year 1889, from the list drawn up by the late Bursar, G. W. Kaye, and printed by Fiddes in his *Chapters in the History of . . . Manchester University*, 1851–1914. From 1890, the figures now printed in the present volume were compiled by R. A. Rainford.

A. NOTABLE BENEFACTIONS

This list includes benefactions of £10,000 upwards. It excludes grants from Government and Local Authorities, as well as amounts below £10,000 contributed to the Appeal Funds of 1920 and 1937.

Donor	Date	Purpose	Amount (£)
John Owens	1850	Foundation of Owens College.	96,654
Manchester Natural History Society	1871–74	Contribution to Building Fund.	5,000
		Contribution to Endowment of Museum.	14,589
E. R. Langworthy	1874	Endowment of Professorship of Experimental Physics.	10,000
Charles Clifton	1875	Mechanical Arts and Engineering.	21,571
C. F. Beyer	1877	Professorships in Science.	100,243
Thomas Wrigley	1881	General Purposes.	10,000
Asa Lees	1883	*do.*	10,000
Abel Heywood	1887	Education of Women.	10,000

Donor	Date	Purpose	Amount (£)
Residuary Legatees of Sir Joseph Whitworth, Bt.	1887	Library and General Purposes.	(Property valued at) 10,000
do.	1888	Building Fund.	25,000
do.	1888	Furnishing Fund.	2,500
do.	1888	Augmentation of Museum Endowment Fund.	10,000
John Rylands	1889	General Purposes.	10,000
Residuary Legatees of Sir Joseph Whitworth, Bt.	1890	Hospital and Medical School.	(Estate costing) 27,700
Edward Schunck	1895	Chemical Research.	20,333
R. C. Christie	1895	Christie Library.	23,000
John Rylands	1898 (Bequest)	General Purposes.	10,964
J. P. Thomasson	1898	Physical Laboratory Building Fund.	10,000
(a) R. C. Christie, R. D. Darbishire, E. Tootal Broadhurst and J. C. Brooks	1898	The Firs Estate (35 acres given in two parts by those shown in (a) and (b) opposite).	
(b) E. Donner, N. Clegg and A. Howarth	1902		
R. C. Christie	1901	Erection of a College Hall for Public Ceremonials.	56,839
J. H. Gartside	1903–12	Scholarships in Commerce and Industry. (Discontinued in 1921, and Research Assistantship in Commerce instituted.)	11,633
Mrs. E. A. Rylands	1908–09 (Bequests)	General Purposes: (Owens College). (The University).	25,000 38,000
		Endowment of Faculty of Theology.	12,000
George Harrison	1908 (Bequest)	Applied to endowment of Chair of Botany.	10,012

Donor	Date	Purpose	Amount (£)
Professor Thomas Barker	1908–26 (Bequest)	Chair of Cryptogamic Botany, and Scholarships or Bursaries in Botany or Mathematics.	26,115
Andrew Carnegie .	1909	New Chemical Laboratory.	10,000
R. C. Christie . .	1911 (Bequest)	Christie Library.	10,000
E. S. Massey . .	1911–12 (Bequest)	Applied for endowment of Chair of Electro-Technics.	10,420
J. E. Taylor . .	1912	General Purposes (later applied for endowment of Chair of English Literature).	20,000
John Hall . .	1913	Professorships and Scholarships in both Chemistry and Philosophy, and the Sir Samuel Hall Oration.	36,014
Professor D. J. Leech	1918–21 (Bequests)	Chair of Materia Medica and Therapeutics.	10,793
Sir James E. Jones .	1919	Ellis Llwyd Jones Lectureship. Ellis Llwyd Jones Hall (and also cost of conversion of the property—amount unknown).	11,360 4,469
Jesse Haworth . .	1923–24	The purposes of the Museum.	30,000
Robert Ottley . .	1929	Commercial Education.	10,000
Royal Botanical and Horticultural Society of Manchester	1935	Research and Instruction in Horticulture.	66,585
Samuel Gratrix, Snr.	1936 (Bequest)	To endow Scholarships.	51,042
J. E. Holt . .	1935 (Bequest)	Scholarships for Medical Students. (Amount received in 1938–39.)	22,542
Sir Robert McDougall	1938–39	Appeal Fund (1937).	12,081
Imperial Chemical Industries, Ltd.	1938–39	*do.*	10,000
Sir Samuel Turner .	1938–39	Dental School and Hospital.	99,000
H. P. Turner . .	1938–39	Appeal Fund (1937).	10,000

Donor	Date	Purpose	Amount (£)
Lewis's Ltd. . .	1944–45	" Woolton Hall " (£5,000 p.a. for 7 years).	35,000
Professor S. Alexander	1945 (Bequest of residuary estate)	Second Chair of Philosophy. (Amount received to 31/7/45.)	10,098
Sir Robert McDougall	1945	Physical Education Centre (Drill Hall, Burlington Street —costing)	9,000
		Arthur McDougall Fund. *Note.*—Sir Robert McDougall also gave the University property in Grafton Street, and made contributions to many University activities, especially the Differential Analyser Research.	34,449
Nuffield Foundation .	1943–44	£3,000 p.a. for 5 years for Chair of Neurology.	15,000
The Needham Family (often anonymously)	1935–45	Needham Family Fund (including " Fair Oak ", Didsbury).	10,750
Lord Simon of Wythenshawe	1943–44	Social Sciences.	27,500
Dr. A. H. Worthington	1945 (Bequest)	To be applied by Council.	26,016
D. F. Pilkington .	1945	Sybil Mary Pilkington Fellowship.	10,000
Miss Edith Hamer .	1944–45 (Bequest)	Scholarships.	25,471
Professor H. M. Hallsworth	1943–45	Research in Political Economy and Administration.	22,991
Alfred Haworth .	1946	To be applied by Council.	60,000
Nuffield Foundation .	1945	Department of Occupational Health (over 10 years).	70,000
do.	1946	Research by Physics Department (over 5 years).	20,000
do.	1948	Department of Rheumatism Research (over 10 years).	100,000

Donor	Date	Purpose	Amount (£)
Dr. Wm. Walker .	1948	Research Scholarship in relation to diseases of women and to obstetrics in St. Mary's Hospital.	16,000 (Approx.)
Sir Richard Needham	1949 (Bequest, including part of residuary estate)	(1) John Stopford Fellowship (2) Scholarships. (3) Foundation and equipment of a library at Needham Hall.	12,000 (Approx.)
J. H. Gartside. .	1950 (Bequest)	To be applied at the discretion of the University.	21,500
Miss Carrie Delaney	1950	To be applied at the discretion of the University.	10,000

The total amount given to the University from the beginning of Owens College to the end of the session 1949–50, excluding grants from the Government and Local Authorities and gifts in kind, has exceeded £3,000,000.

B. COMPARATIVE TABLE OF INCOME FROM 1852 TO 1950

Year ending 31st July	Total Income	Fees from Students—Tuition, Examination and Graduation		Government Grant exclusive of Grants for Services Rendered		Grants from Local Authorities		Income from Investments—General and Special Funds		Other Income	
		Amount	% of Total	Amount	% of Total	Amount	% of Total	Amount	% of Total	Amount	% of Total
	£	£		£		£		£		£	
1852	3,240	699	21·57	—	—	—	—	—	—	—	—
1853	3,696	872	23·59	—	—	—	—	—	—	—	—
1854	3,572	961	26·9	—	—	—	—	—	—	—	—
1855	3,469	735	21·18	—	—	—	—	—	—	—	—
1856	3,441	601	17·46	—	—	—	—	—	—	—	—
1857	3,517	604	17·17	—	—	—	—	—	—	—	—
1858	3,619	520	14·36	—	—	—	—	—	—	—	—
1859	3,900	834	21·38	—	—	—	—	—	—	—	—
1860	3,871	883	22·81	—	—	—	—	—	—	—	—
1861	4,318	1,077	24·94	—	—	—	—	—	—	—	—
1862	4,517	1,345	29·77	—	—	—	—	—	—	—	—
1863	4,804	1,559	32·45	—	—	—	—	—	—	—	—
1864	5,090	1,870	36·73	—	—	—	—	—	—	—	—
1865	5,584	2,341	41·92	—	—	—	—	—	—	—	—
1866	5,446	1,930	35·43	—	—	—	—	—	—	—	—
1867	5,411	2,099	38·79	—	—	—	—	—	—	—	—
1868	6,079	2,685	44·16	—	—	—	—	—	—	—	—
1869	6,817	3,334	48·90	—	—	—	—	—	—	—	—
1870	7,597	3,506	46·14	—	—	—	—	—	—	—	—
1871	9,129	4,148	45·43	—	—	—	—	—	—	—	—
1872	9,811	4,506	45·92	—	—	—	—	—	—	—	—
1873	13,089	6,903	52·73	—	—	—	—	—	—	—	—

1874	13,787	7,716	55·96	—	—	—	—	—	—	—	—
1875	15,916	7,985	50·16	—	—	—	—	—	—	—	—
1876	18,141	8,842	48·74	—	—	—	—	—	—	—	—
1877	18,602	9,292	49·95	—	—	—	—	—	—	—	—
1878	20,093	8,930	44·44	—	—	—	—	—	—	—	—
1879	21,685	10,659	49·15	—	—	—	—	—	—	—	—
1880	21,398	10,970	51·26	—	—	—	—	—	—	—	—
1881	21,719	10,304	47·44	—	—	—	—	—	—	—	—
1882	24,327	11,298	46·44	—	—	—	—	—	—	—	—
1883	24,651	11,568	46·92	—	—	—	—	—	—	—	—
1884	25,644	12,500	48·74	—	—	—	—	—	—	—	—
1885	25,564	11,956	46·76	—	—	—	—	—	—	—	—
1886	23,800	11,261	47·31	—	—	—	—	—	—	—	—
1887	25,449	11,373	44·68	—	—	—	—	—	—	—	—
1888	28,392	12,322	43·39	—	—	—	—	—	—	—	—
1889	29,268	13,039	44·5	—	—	—	—	—	—	—	—
1890	31,337	13,602	43·4	2,250	7·2	—	—	14,035	44·8	1,450	4·6
1891	31,455	13,596	43·2	1,800	5·7	—	—	14,058	44·7	2,001	6·4
1892	32,127	14,262	44·4	1,800	5·6	1,000	3·1	14,040	43·7	1,025	3·2
1893	32,964	14,435	43·8	1,800	5·5	1,400	4·2	14,424	43·8	905	2·7
1894	33,638	15,766	46·9	1,800	5·3	1,000	3·0	14,035	41·7	1,037	3·1
1895	34,257	15,605	45·5	1,840	5·4	1,400	4·1	14,384	42·0	1,028	3·0
1896	34,834	16,505	47·4	1,920	5·5	1,150	3·3	14,190	40·7	1,069	3·1
1897	33,988	16,002	47·1	1,350	4·0	1,300	3·8	14,401	42·3	935	2·8
1898	37,437	16,786	44·8	4,375	11·9	950	2·5	13,920	37·1	1,406	3·7
1899	35,546	16,993	47·8	3,500	9·8	950	2·7	12,964	36·5	1,139	3·2
1900	36,801	17,407	47·3	3,500	9·5	950	2·6	13,432	36·5	1,512	4·1
1901	37,887	18,221	48·1	3,500	9·2	950	2·5	13,667	36·1	1,549	4·1
1902	38,904	17,910	46·0	3,500	9·0	1,050	2·7	14,249	36·6	2,195	5·7
1903	41,278	18,079	43·8	3,500	8·5	1,150	2·8	15,697	38·0	2,852	6·9
1904	44,619	20,114	45·1	3,500	7·8	1,850	4·2	16,521	37·0	2,634	5·9
1905	59,155	22,903	38·7	8,625	14·6	5,250	8·9	17,477	29·5	4,900	8·3

Year ending 31st July	Total Income	Fees from Students—Tuition, Examination and Graduation		Government Grant exclusive of Grants for Services Rendered		Grants from Local Authorities		Income from Investments—General and Special Funds		Other Income	
		Amount	% of Total	Amount	% of Total	Amount	% of Total	Amount	% of Total	Amount	% of Total
	£	£		£		£		£		£	
1906	67,974	24,919	36·7	15,500	22·8	5,200	7·6	17,470	25·7	4,885	7·2
1907	67,879	24,269	35·8	14,000	20·6	5,100	7·5	18,546	27·3	5,964	8·8
1908	67,357	24,333	36·1	13,500	20·0	5,150	7·7	18,247	27·1	6,127	9·1
1909	73,142	26,924	36·8	14,000	19·1	5,250	7·2	20,696	28·3	6,272	8·6
1910	74,804	28,136	37·6	14,000	18·7	5,300	7·1	22,567	30·2	4,801	6·4
1911	74,220	27,710	37·3	14,500	19·6	5,300	7·1	21,195	28·6	5,515	7·4
1912	78,640	27,150	34·5	20,875	26·6	5,300	6·7	17,993	22·9	7,322	9·3
1913	81,807	26,810	32·8	19,500	23·8	5,300	6·5	20,197	24·7	10,000	12·2
1914	81,288	26,785	33·0	19,500	24·0	5,300	6·5	20,643	25·4	9,060	11·1
1915	76,008	22,076	29·0	19,500	25·7	6,050	8·0	20,380	26·8	8,002	10·5
1916	79,066	19,993	25·3	5,000 special } 19,500	31·0	6,050	7·6	18,663	23·6	9,860	12·5
1917	72,394	18,065	24·9	19,500	26·9	6,050	8·4	18,360	25·4	10,419	14·4
1918	73,494	18,081	24·6	19,500	26·5	6,050	8·2	19,213	26·2	10,650	14·5
1919	88,672	27,403	30·9	24,875	28·1	6,050	6·8	19,609	22·1	10,735	12·1
1920	125,878	48,681	38·7	40,000	31·8	6,050	4·8	21,195	16·8	9,952	7·9
1921	153,312	67,893	44·3	42,250	27·5	7,650	5·0	23,274	15·2	12,245	8·0
1922	183,282	74,766	40·8	56,000	30·5	11,650	6·4	37,441	20·4	3,425	1·9
1923	183,244	71,178	38·9	56,000	30·6	11,900	6·5	40,577	22·1	3,589	1·9
1924	182,754	68,667	37·6	56,000	30·7	12,650	6·9	40,996	22·4	4,441	2·4
1925	185,379	62,583	33·7	56,000	30·2	12,965	7·0	46,085	24·9	7,746	4·2
1926	201,356	65,574	32·6	69,000	34·3	13,865	6·9	42,368	21·0	10,549	5·2

Year											
1927	203,575	67,553	33·2	69,000	33·9	16,015	7·9	41,517	20·4	9,490	4·6
1928	224,564	69,433	30·9	69,000	30·7	17,515	7·8	44,887	20·0	23,729	10·6
1929	225,282	74,600	33·1	69,000	30·7	17,865	7·9	46,125	17·8	23,692	10·5
1930	234,868	75,430	32·1	51* 69,000	29·4	18,100	7·7	47,748	20·3	24,539	10·5
1931	259,785	78,278	30·1	1,305* 81,000	31·7	20,100	7·8	52,024	20·0	27,078	10·4
1932	262,310	80,269	30·6	565* 81,000	31·1	20,100	7·7	50,931	19·4	29,445	11·2
1933	260,076	81,677	31·4	100* 81,000	31·2	18,800	7·2	49,858	19·2	28,641	11·0
1934	267,224	83,532	31·3	76* 81,000	30·3	18,800	7·0	52,964	19·9	30,852	11·5
1935	275,318	84,921	30·9	60* 81,000	29·4	19,105	6·9	55,696	20·2	34,536	12·6
1936	273,982	83,219	30·4	121* 81,000	29·6	19,105	7·0	56,335	20·5	34,202	12·5
1937	289,657	75,354	26·0	53* 93,500	32·3	26,855	9·3	58,772	20·3	35,123	12·1
1938	295,695	74,463	25·2	123* 93,500	31·6	27,810	9·4	58,777	19·9	41,022	13·9
1939	291,188	73,917	25·4	30* 93,500	32·1	28,460	9·8	57,876	19·9	37,405	12·8
1940	292,649	73,440	25·1	3,631* 93,500	33·2	28,510	9·7	54,496	18·6	39,072	13·4
1941	286,506	70,292	24·6	4* 93,500	32·6	28,460	9·9	53,518	18·7	40,732	14·2
1942	290,630	75,971	26·1	13* 93,500	32·2	28,460	9·8	50,958	17·5	41,728	14·4
1943	294,221	77,674	26·4	93,500	31·8	28,460	9·7	51,463	17·5	43,124	14·6

* Government Grant—Non-recurrent.

Year ending 31st July	Total Income	Fees from Students—Tuition, Examination and Graduation		Government Grant exclusive of Grants for Services Rendered		Grants from Local Authorities		Income from Investments—General and Special Funds		Other Income	
		Amount	% of Total	Amount	% of Total	Amount	% of Total	Amount	% of Total	Amount	% of Total
	£	£		£		£		£		£	
1944	297,449	74,546	25·1	93,500 21,861*}	31·4	28,460	9·6	53,941	18·1	47,002	15·8
1945	326,826	82,464	25·2	93,500 19,500*}	35·3	28,460	8·7	52,766	16·2	47,775	14·6
1946	448,700	95,022	21·2	193,700	47·5	29,360	6·5	57,520	12·8	53,598	12·0
1947	649,939	144,485	22·2	361,600	55·6	29,260	4·5	60,374	9·3	54,220	8·4
1948	790,617	163,838	20·7	477,225	60·4	30,410	3·8	63,347	8·0	55,797	7·1
1949	859,544	170,911	19·8	543,004	63·2	29,910	3·5	65,060	7·6	50,659	5·9
1950	1,025,871	172,080	16·8	717,167	69·9	32,410	3·2	61,150	6·0	43,064	4·1

* Government Grant—Non-recurrent.

APPENDIX IV

ADMISSION OF WOMEN TO FULL UNIVERSITY STATUS

(Reprinted from Introduction by E. Fiddes to Mrs. Tylecote's volume, " The Education of Women at Manchester University 1883 to 1933 ")

WHEN John Owens founded the college, which bears his name, he made no provision for the education of women. He stated in his will that it was his " earnest desire and general object to found . . . an institution for providing or aiding the means of instructing and improving young persons of the male sex " in university subjects.

This change was not effected all at once. It slowly developed through a series of stages which occupied in all some thirty years. There were three great obstacles : first, there was the legal prohibition in John Owens' will ; then there was the defective condition of women's education ; thirdly, there was a strong public opinion opposed to the higher education of women, especially if it was given to men and women in the same classrooms.

To summarise the various stages by which these obstacles were overcome— we have the Acts of Parliament of 1870 and 1871 which removed the legal barrier against admission to Owens College, and the Charter of the Victoria University in 1880 which placed men and women on an equal footing. Then between 1871 and 1883 there were various attempts to give women higher education without admitting them as members of the College or the University. In 1883 they were admitted to membership as students but under strict limitations which were only gradually removed, till almost full equality between the sexes was reached at the end of the century.

When John Owens made his will in 1845 it is highly unlikely that he considered the inclusion of women in his college as a possibility. What he was anxious about was freedom from sectarian tests. This was very much a live issue in the 'fifties in Manchester. The question of women's education was not.

Higher education presupposes a good secondary education, and in Manchester, as indeed all over England, the secondary education of girls cried out for reform. One need not discuss this in detail. There is abundance of literature

153

on the subject. It is more pertinent to ask why the question of reform became urgent about 1850. Since 1750 two potent agents of change had been at work. One was the theory of Natural Rights which found political expression in the American and French Revolutions. The other, perhaps more potent still, was the great social changes which followed what is usually called the Industrial Revolution. The wealth and the power of the middle classes had greatly increased, and with wealth and power came greater leisure and greater responsibilities. But the majority of the middle classes still clung to the limitation of girls' education which satisfied a previous generation. Beyond these limits, education, they thought, was positively harmful. As Mark Pattison put it in his report to the Schools Enquiry Commission, " An average man of the middle classes prefers a woman who is less educated to one who is more. The preference of a man for a less cultivated woman arises from his own want of culture. Culture has not kept pace with wealth." In the last sentence Mark Pattison summed up the situation. It certainly was true of Lancashire and the North of England. Nowhere had there been greater social changes and nowhere consequently was there greater need for educational reform.

It would of course be a wild exaggeration to say that all the girls' schools in the country were inefficient. But a large section of the schoolmistresses themselves were fully aware of the deficiencies of their profession. Over five hundred had signed a memorandum in the 'sixties on the need of higher education for women who intended to be teachers. Governesses, the alternative to schools, are held up by the novelists of the nineteenth century to contempt or sympathy as drudges, intriguers or sycophants, though it is hard to believe that there were many as able and unscrupulous as Becky Sharpe or as silly and sentimental as Jane Eyre. But many of the wealthier families of the Industrial Revolution, especially in the second generation, set far too high a value on their daughters' education to entrust it to such inferior instruments. They chose governesses and tutors of real learning and capacity to teach.

But making every allowance, the state of girls' education was bad enough. The movement for reform began about the middle of the century with the foundation of Bedford College and Queen's College, but it did not make much progress in the North of England till the 'sixties. The great impetus came from the appointment of the Schools Enquiry Commission in 1864. The report presented a grave indictment of women's education. The defects were summed up as follows : " Want of thoroughness and foundation, want of system, slovenliness and showy superficiality, inattention to rudiments, undue time given to accomplishments and these not taught intelligently or in any scientific manner, want of organisation."

If we turn to the Lancashire report, which is specially germane to our purpose, we find these defects amply illustrated. This report was drawn up by

THE ARTS BUILDING, 1919

James Bryce, afterwards Lord Bryce. It is severe—perhaps too severe, " caustic " is the word used by the Commissioners themselves. Bryce admitted that nearly all schoolmistresses were doing their duty carefully and honestly and singled out some really good schools, but with every allowance his condemnation was sweeping. Organisation, teaching and curriculum were all bad. There were almost no endowments for the secondary education of girls. In all England there were 572 endowed secondary schools for boys with an attendance of 36,000, and only 14 such schools for girls with an attendance of about 1,100. In Lancashire there were no endowed schools for girls at all. Education was almost confined to private establishments, and these for the most part had neither good teachers nor a good curriculum. To quote Bryce again : " The two capital defects of the teachers of girls are these : they have not themselves been well taught and they do not know how to teach." There was no doubt that many schoolmistresses had taken to teaching simply for the laudable purpose of keeping alive.

The curriculum was tolerably good in the early stages. Young girls seem to have been educated not less well than boys of the same age. For the older girls there was no lack of subjects—reading, writing, arithmetic, some languages, " general information " and accomplishments like drawing and music. Reading and writing were well taught, arithmetic badly. " General information " was learned by question and answer out of one or other of " the noxious brood of catechisms " resulting in the injection into the mind of an incoherent congeries of items. The " accomplishments " were for ornament and not for the training of the intellect to a keener perception and appreciation. Even in this poor provender exceptional minds might find the beginnings of intellectual nourishment, but it could neither kindle in the average girl a desire for knowledge nor sharpen and intensify her powers. It is surely an exaggeration to say that a girl's education was arranged simply as a bait to trap a possible husband. Reading, writing and arithmetic at all events were necessary for a civilised being. On the other hand, the superficial " accomplishments ", piano strumming, dancing and drawing, " lined in " by the visiting master, seem to have been intended for personal attraction.

Public opinion, however, had long acquiesced in this form of education as natural and proper. To quote Bryce again : " The notion that women had minds as cultivable and as well worth cultivating as men's minds is still regarded by the ordinary British parent as an offensive, not to say revolutionary paradox." And if girls did acquire learning, what would be the effect on their chances of marriage ? Who would marry a Blue ?

There were, however, two obvious flaws in this reasoning, which treated school education at least in its later years simply as a preparation for marriage. It ignored the fact that a proportion of the pupils would not marry. These would leave school without any adequate preparation to earn a livelihood, and if it happened that in after-life they possessed independent means, still their lives would be cramped and impoverished by their want of intellectual training. But was the fashionable school education the best preparation even for married life ? Many of the duties which had to be performed by middle-class women before the Machine Age and which wholesomely occupied them, could now be devolved or simplified. School had done little to give them—married or single—intellectual training and wide interests. They could not occupy their new leisure with profit and happiness.

To go back to Manchester—even before the appointment of the Schools Enquiry Commission there had been some talk of founding a ladies' college, and in 1869 a Manchester Association for Promoting the Higher Education of Women was founded. But there was still no possibility of help from the natural centre of higher learning in the city. John Owens' will still barred the way. It was impossible or unlikely that the advocates of women's education could themselves at that time have effected a change. But they were able to take advantage of a movement which was not primarily concerned with them. By the late 'sixties Owens College had surmounted its early troubles. It had a brilliant staff. It had a wide reputation for learning. The number of students was increasing. It seemed the right time to put it on a sounder footing. It needed a larger number of teachers, a wider curriculum, new buildings. It should have a constitution befitting a university college. To carry out these aims two things were needed— one was money, the other an Act or Acts of Parliament to sanction the constitutional changes. The money was not difficult to raise. Manchester was prosperous in those days after the cloud of the American Civil War had lifted.

Parliamentary sanction was more difficult. There was very properly considerable hesitation before proceeding to alter a trust which had been in operation for barely twenty years and which was carrying out the objects of the founder. Nevertheless the changes were accomplished by a series of legal manœuvres. The conditions of John Owens Trust were drastically revised. By the Act of 1870 a new college was incorporated under the name of the Owens Extension College. It was to hold the funds recently raised. It was to have the constitution of a university college and not merely to be a private trust. Further, it was to have power to incorporate Owens College and after incorporation to take over its name. Under an Act of 1871 the incorporation took place. With a wave of the parliamentary wand the old Owens College disappeared and, hey-presto ! a reconstituted and reformed Owens College took its place.

Whatever criticisms might be offered to these proceedings by strict legalists there is no doubt they met with general approval. In particular, the power to admit women, which was permissive and not mandatory, had been carefully brought to the attention of the new subscribers. The reconstituted college was therefore based on funds, the larger part of which were given by persons who at least consented that it should have the power to admit women.   But the Charity Commissioners to whom a scheme had to be submitted desired further safeguards. In particular, they insisted on two conditions.   One was that the power to admit women should not be exercised unless the governing body had sufficient pecuniary means for the purpose after adequate provision had been made for the instruction of male applicants.   The other was that due arrangements should be made for securing the effective separation of the students of different sexes when attending for the purposes of instruction.   As regards the first proviso, at no time has it been suggested that the women were crowding out the men.   As for the second proviso, no one has defined what is meant by effective separation.   It was obviously susceptible of various interpretations, and what was actually discussed was whether women should be taught in the same classrooms as men.   This was the real storm centre for a long time.

The party of resistance held that the proper line of demarcation was Oxford Road.   West of it were the college buildings.   Here the men were taught.   East of it there was a house in Brunswick Street which became the first abode of women students.

The other party held that a classroom was hardly a probable or even a possible place for unseemly behaviour of the kind envisaged by the alarmists.   Experience has long shown that it is almost inconceivable even with the worst disciplinarians in command, though there were direful prophecies of disaster.

In 1871 John Owens' restriction was gone.   The change had required some effort, and it might have been thought that the college authorities would at once have set to work to consider whether and to what extent women might now be admitted as students, if not to the same classes as the men, at least to recognised classes of their own.   But twelve years had to elapse before women were admitted as college students at all.   It was plain that only a permissive clause could have been carried.   It was also plain that the predominant party in the college, headed by the Principal, were in no hurry to make use of the permission.   But the other party—which included men like Ward and Adamson in the Senate and Robert Darbishire in the Council—were not disposed to let the matter drop, and the women themselves were naturally becoming impatient.

In April, 1875, a letter appeared in the *Manchester Examiner* asking for the opening of classes to women.   The writer referred to the Principal's emphasis on the importance of separating the sexes and suggested, whether seriously or ironically, that the difficulty might be surmounted by erecting a barrier or lattice midway down the room.   Robert Darbishire continued the correspondence in the *Manchester Guardian*.   The authorities of Owens College, he said, were not Mohammedan priests nor timid or nasty-minded recluses, but fathers and brothers and Christian gentlemen.   Crumbs should not be refused to these dogs, the cultivated young women of Manchester.   Various letters followed.   " A poor hungry wistful waiting dog" pleaded for admission. "Governor" replied he would be delighted to meet the wistful waiting dog and examine her, but the admission of women would be unfair to those who wished to use the college as a place of quiet study. Whereupon "Dog Kicked" complained of trivial sarcasm and demanded justice.

This exchange of courtesy was no doubt very witty. It was not, however, either edifying or profitable. Unfortunately it was characteristic of more than one of these controversies. The men pooh-poohed, often with little taste, the claims of the women as a sort of bad joke. The women often began with serious arguments and then ended by losing their tempers.

In April, 1877, an attempt to get a definite pronouncement in favour of the admission of women was made at a Court meeting. Dr. Cowie, the Dean of Manchester, moved a resolution, "that the Court is prepared to sanction the teaching of women in the College under such regulations as to subjects, classes, discipline and other matters as may be approved by the Council and Senate". To this an amendment was moved. It expressed great sympathy with the higher education of women, but the Court, it went on to say, was not prepared to sanction the principle of mixed education, believing that this would be at once opposed to the true educational interests of students of either sex and out of harmony with the sentiments and usages of society. The amendment was carried by twenty-one votes to five.

But uncompromising opposition was no longer possible. The reform of the girls' schools was steadily going on. In 1874 the Manchester High School for Girls was opened. The Manchester Association for Promoting the Higher Education of Women had been in existence since 1869. So some very cautious experiments were made. In the session 1875–76 women were admitted to a carefully selected list of classes. These were Comparative Philology, English Literature, Physics and Political Economy. The basis of this selection remains a mystery. For professors in other than these subjects were quite ready to admit the women to their classes. But even in the selected classes women were not allowed to attend as students but as visitors, and to mark their being there on sufferance they were denied the privilege of paying fees.

A more definite step was taken in 1877. A Manchester and Salford College for Women was established. It had no organic connection with Owens College, but it was in close relations with it. On its committee were prominent members of the Council and Senate. Most of its teaching was given by professors and lecturers of Owens College. A Board appointed by the Senate conducted its examinations and awarded its certificates. It was supported partly by fees, partly by contributions. It was situated in a house near the college, a gloomy and cramped home of learning indeed, but still a beginning. The movement had to be content with this half-way measure for the next few years. The energies of Owens College were fully occupied in the later 'seventies by a vital question. A determined effort was being made to carry out a long-cherished scheme—the establishment of a university in Manchester.

The result for the time being was only partially successful. It was hoped to convert Owens College into the University of Manchester. That was not accomplished till 1903. In the 'seventies the opposition of other bodies was too strong. As a compromise the Victoria University was established in 1880. It was federal in character with separate constituent colleges, of which Owens College was the first.

The Charter of the new University fully recognised the equality of women students. " The University ", ran Clause IV, " shall have power to grant and confer all such degrees and other distinctions as now or at any time hereafter can be granted and conferred by any other University in our United Kingdom of Great Britain and Ireland to and on all persons male or female who shall have pursued a regular course of study in a College in the University and shall submit themselves for examination."

The Charter of 1880 did not give powers to the University to confer degrees in Medicine. This defect was remedied in 1883 by a supplementary charter, and in it again all qualified persons male or female were put on an equal footing.

The position was now more anomalous than ever. The Acts of 1870 and 1871 had permitted the admission of women to Owens College. The Charter of 1880 had thrown open all degrees of the University to women on the same conditions as to men. But one necessary qualification for a degree was membership of a constituent college. Owens was at that time the one constituent college, and Owens resolutely refused to open its doors to women. Under these circumstances a renewal of the agitation was inevitable, and at the end of 1880 a vigorous controversy raged in the Press. The letters have been reprinted and a copy of the reprint is in the University Library. It is entitled : Owens College *v*. Ladies. Letters of Amanda and others and some by Amans ; Printers, Menes, Tekel and Pharsin. The chief protagonists were, for the women, Amanda, and for the men, Amans, but there were a dozen others, for example, " Sibyl ", " Rosa ", " Student ", " Observer ", " Lancashire Woman ", " M.D.", while one or two sensibly signed their own names, like " Ursula Bright ".

Amanda began the correspondence with a long letter complaining of the continued exclusion of women in spite of the University Charter. Unfortunately she thought it necessary to commence her first letter with a rather cloudy display of classical learning, but she stated her main arguments very well. She pointed out in particular the great waste of time involved in the repetition of lectures in Brunswick Street, after they had already been given in Owens College. The danger of intellectual or physical strain was the concern of the students themselves or their parents, not of the college. She believed a new age of power, confidence and co-operation between the sexes would result from a common preparation for life. Lastly, Manchester was in danger of falling behind Liverpool, Leeds and Sheffield.

The other supporters of the women mainly emphasised and supplemented Amanda's arguments. Surely lectures given out of touch with the laboratories and the library must be inferior. Striking testimony was quoted from Henry Morley and Stanley Jevons at University College, London, to the good effect of the presence of women in the classes, and there was further evidence from many spheres of life that men and women could work together without evil results.

The other side, in addition to a discharge of small wit, such as enquiring whether Amanda was tall or short, blonde or brunette, and had she much money ? confined themselves to arguing on an *a priori* view of human nature that mixed classes would lead to the most serious and disgraceful scandals. They asked the Professors " if they would like to have the duties of duennas to a set of girl graduates [*sic*] superadded to the already arduous tasks they have to fulfil " ? " M.D." attempted to mediate. There was a danger in association, but it might be overcome. But was it worth while ? Would it not be better for women to work out a scheme of higher education for themselves ? Another writer made the staggering assertion that " the Owens students as a whole do not breathe an atmosphere fit for modest and single-hearted English maidenhood. Over and above the black sheep who will disgrace themselves in every flock there is a floating mass of rowdies." He asked for evidences of the successful working of joint education. Let Amanda arrange for a Town's Meeting to discuss the question. " Then if the thing may be done and the way is clear before us, ring [*sic*] clarions and advance our standards and let us deal one more death blow at the crass levies of the fiend Ignorance and Bigotry her offspring."

There are two points to be noticed in the correspondence. The weight of arguments as well as numbers was in favour of the women, and the point of issue had shifted since the 'sixties. At that time many persons still believed that it was unwise to give higher education to women at all. In the 'eighties no one cared frankly to support that view. The whole debate turned on the advisability of common education with men.

Whatever influence the newspaper controversy had on public opinion, it was obvious, even to the most ardent conservatives, that to refuse indefinitely to admit women after the University Charter had been granted would merely be to stultify themselves. The position had become untenable, but it must be admitted that the garrison retired with all due deliberation and with all the honours of war.

While Amanda and Amans were still exchanging bouquets in the Press, Professor Robert Adamson carried a motion that in the opinion of the Senate it was desirable to admit women students to certain classes in Arts and Science in the University. About the same time the Committee of the Women's College forwarded a memorial to the College Council asking them to take it over and allow its students, if properly qualified, to become candidates for degrees. It was no longer possible, they said, to maintain even the present standard of efficiency.

Many bodies had to be consulted and there were prolonged discussions till at long last in April, 1883, membership of the college was by resolution of the Court opened to women students. There were various conditions. Women were only to be admitted to classes held in Owens College if they were in preparation for the final examinations, or at any rate for the final and intermediate examinations jointly. All others were to be held in Brunswick Street, but these too ranked as preparation for degrees. Moreover, from excess of caution the scheme was only sanctioned for five years in the first instance. During the period the Committee of the Women's College would make an annual payment of £500.

A new point arose almost immediately. Women could now become Owens College students. Did this mean that they were eligible for Owens College scholarships? The instruments of foundation gave no guidance. Discrimination was unnecessary as long as there were only men students. Who could say what the wishes of the founders would have been if they had foreseen the admission of women? A test case arose when a woman applied for the Victoria Scholarship. She was not allowed to compete as the legal position was doubtful, but Mr. Thomas Ashton came to the rescue and offered a special Victoria Scholarship for Women. In 1885 two of the old scholarships and some of the prizes were thrown open.

In 1888 the probationary period of five years expired and there was no hesitation in continuing the scheme. The Council was now empowered to admit women to any lecture class of higher than matriculation grade. They might be admitted to laboratories too, but a special resolution had to be passed in these cases. Scholarships were thrown open unless definitely restricted to men.

One or two other small changes may be mentioned. There was a Department of Evening Classes in the College in which at one time there were many more students than in the regular day classes. From these women had been excluded. It was thought there would be grave danger if they were admitted to classes along with men at the witching hours between say 6 and 8 or even 9 p.m. In the 'nineties the attendances on the evening classes rapidly diminished. Much of the teaching could now be obtained elsewhere, and it was held that the College might reasonably get rid of a burden of elementary instruction which was not its proper business. So the classes were drastically cut down and confined to advanced instruction or at least instruction which could not easily be obtained elsewhere.   To the classes still held after much anxious consideration women were admitted in 1896.   In 1897 the entire range of instruction was now open to women with two exceptions—Engineering and Medicine.   Engineering had not been opened simply because it was not expected that any women would wish to study it.   As soon as one appeared a few years later she was at once admitted.

The other exception is far more important.   A legal title to practice medicine was claimed at the very beginning of the movement for the higher education of women.   The claim met with the most vigorous opposition.   It was as though an attacking army had begun by hurling itself on the enemy where he was most strongly entrenched, for a great body of respectable opinion was genuinely revolted by the idea that women should be allowed to study the human body. Two women succeeded in slipping in by sidedoors which were thereupon bolted and barred against further unwelcome intruders.   This only led to an eight years' campaign under the uncompromising and provocative leadership of Sophia Jex Blake, a campaign marked by resolutions and counter-resolutions of university authorities and licensing bodies, by law suits, by insults from unmannerly students, by a libel action and an Act of Parliament, till at last in 1876 women were entitled to admission to the Medical Register.   In the next twenty years a number of medical schools opened their doors to women.

In 1899 the question was raised in Manchester.   Enquiries were made of the schools where there were already women medical students.   Everywhere assurances were given that discipline had not suffered, nor had the number of men students become less.   The proposal went through with an ease which would have been considered miraculous twenty years before.

The college had now completely reversed its policy since the Court in 1877 affirmed its view that the education of men and women in common was out of harmony with the sentiments and usages of society.   Society had been converted —reluctantly and partially it may be—but serious opposition had died away. Every department of study was now open to women students.   There were still battles to be fought over their admission to the teaching staff, but that will be dealt with later.

EDWARD FIDDES.

THE WHITWORTH HALL.

APPENDIX V

NUMBERS OF STUDENTS

These figures have been supplied by F. P. WALTON, Assistant Registrar. Where the totals which appear in the last column are not the arithmetical addition of the relevant figures in the earlier columns, the discrepancy is due to the inclusion in the earlier columns of students registered in more than one faculty.

Session	Day Students other than in Medicine and Technology			In Medicine			In Technology			Grand Total allowing for Double Entries
	Men	Women	Total	Men	Women	Total	Men	Women	Total	
1851–1852	62	—	62	—	—	—	—	—	—	62
1852–1853	71	—	71	—	—	—	—	—	—	71
1853–1854	71	—	71	—	—	—	—	—	—	71
1854–1855	58	—	58	—	—	—	—	—	—	58
1855–1856	52	—	52	—	—	—	—	—	—	52
1856–1857	33	—	33	—	—	—	—	—	—	33
1857–1858	34	—	34	—	—	—	—	—	—	34
1858–1859	40	—	40	—	—	—	—	—	—	40
1859–1860	57	—	57	—	—	—	—	—	—	57
1860–1861	69	—	69	—	—	—	—	—	—	69
1861–1862	88	—	88	—	—	—	—	—	—	88
1862–1863	108	—	108	—	—	—	—	—	—	108
1863–1864	110	—	110	—	—	—	—	—	—	110
1864–1865	128	—	128	—	—	—	—	—	—	128
1865–1866	113	—	113	—	—	—	—	—	—	113
1866–1867	113	—	113	—	—	—	—	—	—	113
1867–1868	173	—	173	—	—	—	—	—	—	173
1868–1869	210	—	210	—	—	—	—	—	—	210
1869–1870	209	—	209	—	—	—	—	—	—	209

1870–1871	264	—	264	—	—	—	—	—	—	264
1871–1872	327	—	327	—	—	—	—	—	—	327
1872–1873	337	—	337	134	—	134	—	—	—	471
1873–1874	356	—	356	139	—	139	—	—	—	495
1874–1875	375	—	375	143	—	143	—	—	—	518
1875–1876	395	—	395	150	—	150	—	—	—	545
1876–1877	415	—	415	154	—	154	—	—	—	569
1877–1878	418	—	418	162	—	162	—	—	—	580
1878–1879	443	—	443	186	—	186	—	—	—	629
1879–1880	392	—	392	220	—	220	—	—	—	612
1880–1881	417	—	417	216	—	216	—	—	—	633
1881–1882	390	—	390	254	—	254	—	—	—	644
1882–1883	373	—	373	246	—	246	—	—	—	619
1883–1884	400	60	460	276	—	276	—	—	—	736
1884–1885	393	50	443	276	—	276	—	—	—	719
1885–1886	380	66	446	299	—	299	—	—	—	745
1886–1887	364	67	431	283	—	283	—	—	—	714
1887–1888	389	74	463	310	—	310	—	—	—	773
1888–1889	405	68	473	328	—	328	—	—	—	801
1889–1890	410	72	482	329	—	329	—	—	—	811
1890–1891	429	61	490	321	—	321	—	—	—	811
1891–1892	477	81	558	382	—	382	—	—	—	940
1892–1893	507	93	600	345	—	345	—	—	—	945
1893–1894	527	108	635	330	—	330	—	—	—	965
1894–1895	484	108	592	346	—	346	—	—	—	938
1895–1896	566	104	670	322	—	322	—	—	—	992
1896–1897	524	102	626	338	—	338	—	—	—	964
1897–1898	546	99	645	341	—	341	—	—	—	986
1898–1899	528	111	639	355	—	355	—	—	—	994
1899–1900	507	126	633	369	—	369	—	—	—	1,002
1900–1901	506	166	672	369	5	374	—	—	—	1,001
1901–1902	534	172	706	316	4	320	—	—	—	995

Session	Day Students other than in Medicine and Technology			In Medicine			In Technology			Grand Total allowing for Double Entries
	Men	Women	Total	Men	Women	Total	Men	Women	Total	
1902–1903	652	201	853	348	9	357	—	—	—	1,148
1903–1904	643	235	878	354	13	367	—	—	—	1,208
1904–1905	680	253	933	307	12	319	—	—	—	1,252
1905–1906	711	263	974	295	12	307	122	3	125	1,371
1906–1907	704	262	966	311	14	325	164	3	167	1,408
1907–1908	746	302	1,048	312	15	327	148	1	149	1,492
1908–1909	798	325	1,123	327	20	347	160	1	161	1,587
1909–1910	807	328	1,135	350	22	372	189	3	192	1,657
1910–1911	808	312	1,120	357	21	378	214	3	217	1,691
1911–1912	821	330	1,151	306	28	334	201	5	206	1,660
1912–1913	770	320	1,092	340	32	372	244	2	246	1,663
1913–1914	787	328	1,115	272	34	306	278	2	280	1,655
1914–1915	608	329	937	221	35	256	220	2	222	1,415
1915–1916	390	325	715	214	67	281	166	4	170	1,166
1916–1917	301	333	634	224	91	315	148	4	152	1,029
1917–1918	265	345	610	230	123	353	120	9	129	1,031
1918–1919	553	373	926	392	146	538	280	7	287	1,649
1919–1920	1,144	457	1,601	628	143	771	549	12	561	2,775
1920–1921	1,135	508	1,643	607	147	754	492	10	502	2,899
1921–1922	1,120	558	1,678	585	149	734	448	4	452	2,864
1922–1923	1,021	581	1,602	560	145	705	338	1	339	2,646
1923–1924	937	626	1,563	557	128	685	290	—	290	2,538
1924–1925	907	619	1,526	543	107	650	263	—	263	2,439
1925–1926	940	604	1,544	472	98	570	230	—	230	2,344
1926–1927	1,032	586	1,618	495	83	578	240	1	241	2,437

1927–1928	1,086	600	1,686	491	73	564	231	—	231	2,481
1928–1929	1,110	611	1,721	577	85	662	240	2	242	2,625
1929–1930	1,140	596	1,736	599	80	679	250	2	252	2,667
1930–1931	1,183	604	1,787	597	83	680	250	2	252	2,719
1931–1932	1,236	582	1,818	638	89	727	263	3	266	2,811
1932–1933	1,268	595	1,863	668	101	769	296	5	301	2,933
1933–1934	1,326	605	1,931	708	117	825	307	8	315	3,071
1934–1935	1,340	553	1,893	721	129	850	314	5	319	3,062
1935–1936	1,299	511	1,810	722	137	859	297	3	300	2,969
1936–1937	1,183	434	1,617	673	124	797	266	4	270	2,684
1937–1938	1,211	426	1,637	663	137	800	288	4	292	2,729
1938–1939	1,208	452	1,660	666	127	793	318	3	321	2,774
1939–1940	1,095	460	1,555	651	149	800	286	2	288	2,643
1940–1941	965	464	1,429	606	155	761	241	1	242	2,432
1941–1942	1,040	512	1,552	628	176	804	281	5	286	2,642
1942–1943	977	571	1,548	601	186	787	309	6	315	2,650
1943–1944	863	623	1,486	582	195	777	294	9	303	2,566
1944–1945	920	719	1,639	556	220	776	322	5	327	2,742
1945–1946	1,354	934	2,288	660	235	895	388	8	396	3,579
1946–1947	2,122	1,081	3,203	825	235	1,060	625	10	635	4,898
1947–1948	2,643	1,097	3,740	803	250	1,053	767	10	777	5,570
1948–1949	3,036	1,023	4,059	746	253	999	857	11	868	5,926
1949–1950	3,073	995	4,068	772	238	1,010	852	12	864	5,942

APPENDIX VI

PHYSICAL EXPANSION: EXTENSION OF SITE, AND ERECTION OF NEW BUILDINGS

An attempt has been made to represent this graphically by plans taken from Ordnance Survey maps. Three of these are reproduced overleaf. The dates of erection of new buildings are entered at appropriate places on the plans.

The plot purchased in 1870 by Owens College was bounded on the north by Coupland Street, on the east by Oxford Road, on the south by Burlington Street. On the west, there was no street to mark the complete boundary. From Coupland Street the boundary line ran along Higher Chatham Street, then through private property to a point in Burlington Street between Wright Street and Oxford Street.

Plan 1 (p. 170).—The site in 1888, before it crossed Coupland Street on the north and Burlington Street on the south.

Plan 2 (p. 171).—The site in 1911, showing the invasion across Coupland Street and Burlington Street, and the extension to Lloyd Street on the west.

Plan 3 (p. 172).—The site in 1950, showing the closure of Coupland Street, and the extension of the north boundary to Bridge Street; the occupation of Lime Grove as far as Wright Street on the west, and the extension beyond Lime Grove to the south towards Leamington Street; on the east, the Oxford Road front was extended in both a northerly and a southerly direction; on the west side, the boundary ran from the crossing of Bridge Street and Lloyd Street to the junction of Lloyd Street and Burlington Street, along Burlington Street for a short distance, then along the east side of Wright Street, though a few plots on the west side were acquired.

The 1950 plan shows the location of two other major units of the Oxford Road site: (1) The McDougall Centre (Physical Education, University Training Corps, Swimming Bath, Gymnasium, etc). This is situated along Burlington Street to the west of Lloyd Street. (2) The Dover Street Building (formerly the home of the Manchester High School for Girls) houses Education, Law, Economics, Social Sciences and Music; and an annexe to it forms the Arthur Worth-

168

ington Hall which is fitted for concerts and dramatic performances : the block is along Dover Street some 200 yards from Oxford Road.

The departments of Pathology and Bacteriology are located in York Place, near the Manchester Royal Infirmary, about 500 yards from the University farther south along the Oxford Road. They are not shown on the plan.

Nearer to the University by some 100 yards from the Infirmary, and on the opposite side of the Oxford Road, a building recently acquired, nos. 316–324 Oxford Road, will, by 1951, house the University Press and the Appointments Board. This, also, is not shown on the plan.

M*

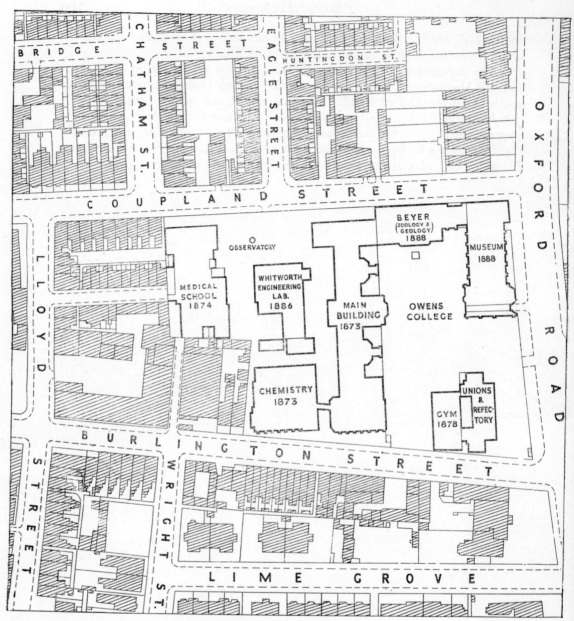

PLAN OF THE UNIVERSITY, 1888

(Scale 1″ to 133′)

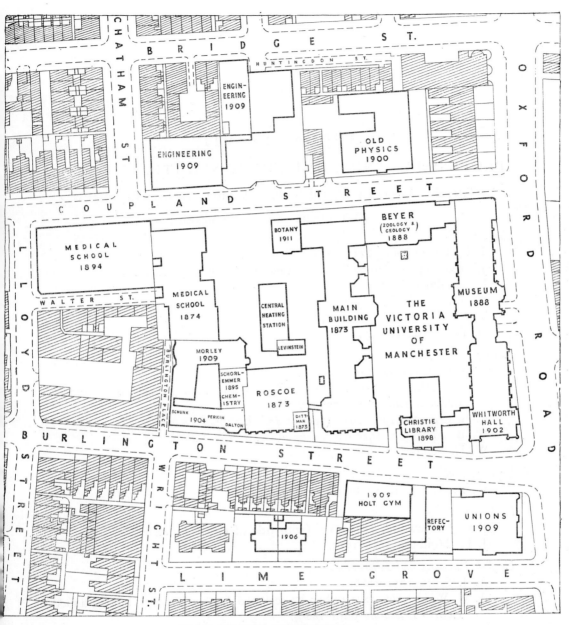

PLAN OF THE UNIVERSITY, 1911
(Scale 1″ to 133′)

APPENDIX VII

PROFESSORS AND MEMBERS OF SENATE, 1851–1951

This list has been compiled by F. P. Walton, Assistant Registrar.

(P–T means part-time professor.)

Greek :

J. G. Greenwood, 1851–1885.

J. Strachan, 1885–1907 (also of *Comparative Philology*, 1890–1907).

R. M. Burrows, 1908–1913.

W. M. Calder, 1913–1930.

T. B. L. Webster, 1931–1948.

H. D. Westlake, 1949–.

Latin :

J. G. Greenwood, 1851–1869.

A. S. Wilkins, 1869–1903 (also of *Comparative Philology*, 1873–1890 and of *Classical Literature*, 1903–1905).

R. S. Conway, 1903–1929 (and of *Indo-European Philology*).

W. B. Anderson, 1929–1936 (see also *Imperial Latin*).

W. H. Semple, 1937–.

Imperial Latin :

W. B. Anderson, 1913–1929.

Hellenistic Greek :

J. G. Greenwood, 1885–1889 (with title of *Greek Testament*).

J. H. Moulton, 1908–1917.

English Language and Literature :

A. J. Scott, 1851–1866.

A. W. Ward, 1866–1875 (when he resigned *English Language*, but continued *English Literature* until 1889).

English Language :

T. N. Toller, 1880–1903.

W. J. Sedgefield, 1913–1931.

PLAN OF THE UNIVERSITY, 1950

NEW DENTAL HOSPITAL 1940

LLOYD ST

BRIDGE ST.

ENGINEERING 1909
ELEC ENG 1949
ELECTRICAL ENGINEERING 1912
METALLURGY 1948
MUSEUM EXT. 1927

ENGINEERING 1909
NEW PHYSICS 1932
PHYSICS
PHYSICS 1900
MUSEUM 1912

MEDICAL SCHOOL 1894
MEDICAL SCHOOL 1874
BOTANY 1911
1888
ZOOLOGY & GEOLOGY 1888
MUSEUM 1888

OXFORD RD.

DIXON LABS 1946
CENTRAL HEATING STATION
MAIN BUILDING 1873

MORLEY 1909
1895
CHEMISTRY 1873
WHITWORTH HALL 1902

LAPWORTH LAB 1950
1904
CHRISTIE LIBRARY 1898

TO THE McDOUGALL CENTRE. 140 YDS. SEE INSET.

BURLINGTON ST.

ROBINSON LABS. CHEMISTRY 1950

No.8 PRESS FLUID MOTION
No.10

THE ARTS LIBRARY 1937

DEAF EDUCATION
STAFF HOUSE 1938
THE REFECTORIES
THE UNIONS 1909 1936

LIME GROVE

WRIGHT ST.
LLOYD ST.

THE ARTS BUILDING. 1919
M.U.A.S.
ARCHITECTURE 1922

ENGLISH 1920
SEMITICS

LIBRARY EXT 1949
No.7
ARTS EXTENSION 1948

OXFORD RD.

LEAMINGTON AV.
BLOSSOM ST.

GEOGRAPHY

ECONOMIC RESEARCH

GERMAN

DUCIE ST.

LEAMINGTON ST.

ACKERS ST.

BURLINGTON ST.

FIVES
SQUASH
SENIOR TRAINING CORPS
SWIMMING BATH

FROM THE UNIVERSITY.

THE McDOUGALL CENTRE 1940
GYMNASIUM

PARK ST.

THE McDOUGALL CENTRE BURLINGTON STREET

BRUNSWICK ST.

EXTRA MURAL AND THEOLOGY

DOVER ST.

DOVER ST. BUILDING. 1947

EDUCATION ECONOMICS MUSIC LAW
1948
ARTHUR WORTHINGTON HALL

RUMFORD ST.

N
W — E
S

SCALE OF FEET
0   50   100   150   200

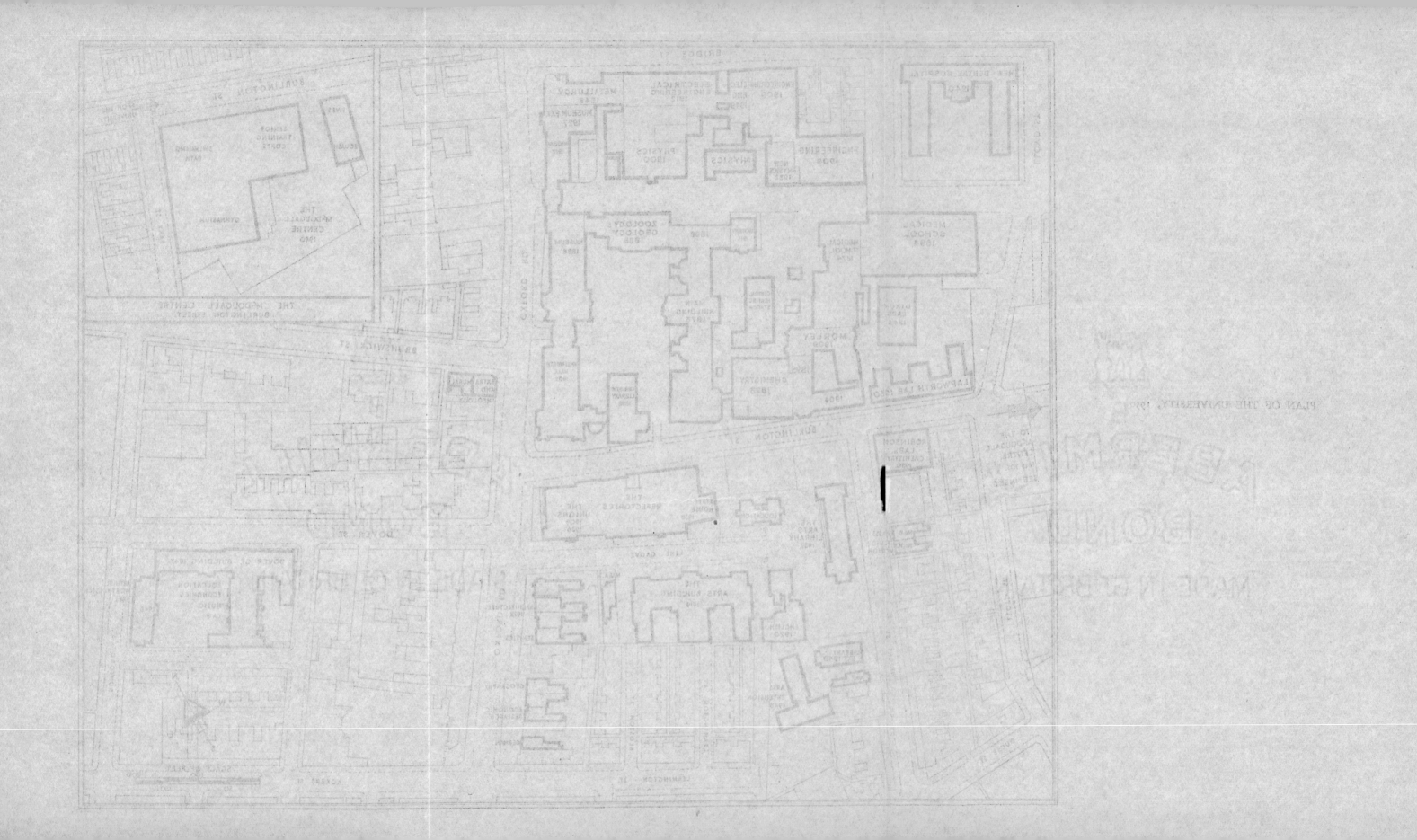

E. V. Gordon, 1931–1938 (with title *English Language and Germanic Philology*).
G. L. Brook, 1945–.

English Literature :
C. H. Herford, 1901–1921.
H. B. Charlton, 1921–.

Modern Languages :
T. Theodores, 1866–1879 (with title *Modern and Oriental Languages*).

French Language and Literature :
V. Kastner, 1895–1909.
L. E. Kastner, 1909–1933.
E. Vinaver, 1933–.

French Language :
J. Orr, 1919–1933.
Mildred K. Pope (with title *French Language and Romance Philology*), 1934–1939.

Romance Philology :
T. B. W. Reid, 1945–.

German and Germanic Philology :
A. Johannson, 1895–1930.

German Language and Literature :
B. Fairley, 1932–1936.
Eliza M. Butler, 1936–1945.
R. Peacock, 1945–.

Russian Language and Literature :
M. V. Trofimov, 1919–1945.
S. Dobrin (with title *Russian Studies*), 1947–.

Italian Studies :
E. G. Gardner, 1920–1923.
P. Rebora, 1923–1932.
M. Praz, 1932–1934.
W. L. Bullock, 1935–1944.

Hebrew :
A. J. Scott, 1851–1860.
T. Theodores, 1860–1884 (with title from 1866 of *Oriental Languages*).

Semitic Languages and Literatures :
H. W. Hogg, 1903–1912.
M. A. Canney, 1912–1934.

Semitic Languages and Literatures—cont.
 E. Robertson, 1934–1945.
 H. H. Rowley, 1945– (with title changed in 1949 to *Hebrew Language and Literature*).

Mesopotamian Studies :
 T. Fish, 1948–.

Arabic :
 J. Robson, 1949–.

Chinese :
 E. H. Parker (P–T), 1901–1926.

History :
 J. G. Greenwood, 1851–1854.
 R. C. Christie, 1854–1866 (also of *Political Economy*, 1855–1866, and of *Jurisprudence and Law*, 1855–1869).
 A. W. Ward, 1866–1897.
 T. F. Tout, *History*, 1890–1902 ; *Mediæval and Modern History*, 1902–1920 ; *History and Director of Advanced Studies*, 1920–1925 ; *in toto* 1890–1925.
 J. Tait (*Ancient and Mediæval History*), 1902–1919.
 G. Unwin (*Economic History*), 1910–1925.
 J. R. B. Muir (*Modern History*), 1914–1921.
 F. M. Powicke (*Mediæval History*), 1919–1928.
 H. W. C. Davis (*Modern History*), 1921–1925.
 J. E. Neale (*Modern History*), 1925–1927.
 E. Fiddes (*Ward Chair of History*), 1926–1931.
 E. F. Jacob (*Mediæval History*), 1929–1944.
 D. Atkinson (*Ancient History*), 1929–.
 L. B. Namier (*Modern History*), 1931–.
 C. R. Cheney (*Mediæval History*), 1945–.
 A. Redford (*Economic History*), 1945–.

Philosophy (until 1896 entitled *Logic and Mental and Moral Philosophy*) :
 A. J. Scott, 1851–1866.
 W. S. Jevons, 1866–1876 (also of *Political Economy*).
 R. Adamson, 1876–1893 (also [to 1882] of *Political Economy*).
 S. Alexander, 1893–1924.
 J. L. Stocks, 1924–1936.
 A. D. Ritchie, 1937–1945.
 Dorothy Emmet, 1946–.

Education :

    H. L. Withers, 1899–1902.

    J. J. Findlay, 1903–1925.

    M. E. Sadler, 1903–1911 (*History and Administration of Education*).

    H. Bompas Smith, 1912–1932.

    J. F. Duff, 1932–1937.

    R. A. C. Oliver, 1938–.

    A. W. G. Ewing (*Education of the Deaf*), 1949–.

    R. D. Waller (*Adult Education*), 1949–.

Political Economy :

    R. C. Christie, 1855–1866 (also of *History*, 1854–1866, and *Jurisprudence and Law*, 1855–1869).

    W. S. Jevons, 1866–1876 (also of *Philosophy*, 1866–1876).

    R. Adamson, 1876–1882 (also of *Philosophy*, 1876–1893).

    J. E. C. Munro, 1882–1890 (also of *Law*, 1882–1892).

    A. W. Flux, 1898–1901.

    Sydney J. Chapman, 1901–1918.

    D. H. Macgregor, 1919–1921.

    Henry Clay (*Political Economy*), 1921–1927 ; (*Social Economics*), 1927–1930.

    G. W. Daniels (*Commerce and Administration*), 1921–1927 ; (*Political Economy*), 1927–1937.

    J. Jewkes (*Social Economics*), 1936–1946 ; (*Political Economy*), 1946–1948.

    J. R. Hicks (*Political Economy*), 1938–1946.

    M. Polanyi (*Social Studies*), 1948– (see also *Chemistry*).

    W. A. Lewis (*Political Economy*), 1947–.

    E. Devons (*Applied Economics*), 1948–.

    A. Henderson (*Economic Theory*), 1949–1950.

Government and Administration :

    W. J. M. Mackenzie, 1948–.

Social Anthropology :

    H. M. Gluckman, 1949–.

Architecture :

    S. H. Capper, 1903–1912.

    A. C. Dickie, 1912–1933.

    R. A. Cordingley, 1933–.

Geography :

    H. J. Fleure, 1930–1944.

    W. Fitzgerald, 1944–1949.

American Studies :
  I. L. Kandel, 1948–1950.

Mathematics :
  A. Sandeman, 1851–1865.
  T. Barker, 1865–1885.
  A. Schuster (*Applied Maths.*), 1881–1888 (see also *Physics*).
  H. Lamb, 1885–1920.
  S. Chapman (*Maths. and Nat. Phil.*), 1919–1924.
  L. J. Mordell (*Pure Maths.*), 1923–1945.
  E. A. Milne (*Applied Maths.*), 1924–1928.
  D. R. Hartree (*Applied Maths.*), 1929–1937 (see also *Physics* and *Engineering*).
  S. Goldstein (*Applied Maths.*), 1945–1950.
  M. H. A. Newman (*Pure Maths.*), 1945–.
  M. S. Bartlett (*Mathematical Statistics*), 1947–.
  M. J. Lighthill (*Applied Maths.*), 1950–.

Physics :
  A. Sandeman, 1851–1860 (see also *Mathematics*).
  R. B. Clifton, 1860–1866.
  W. Jack, 1866–1870.
  Balfour Stewart, 1870–1877.
  T. H. Core, 1870–1905.
  A. Schuster, 1888–1907 (see also *Mathematics*).
  E. Rutherford, 1907–1919.
  W. L. Bragg, 1919–1937.
  D. R. Hartree (*Theoretical Physics*), 1937–1945 (see also *Mathematics* and *Engineering*).
  P. M. S. Blackett, 1937–.
  L. Rosenfeld (*Theoretical Physics*), 1947–.

Crystallography :
  H. A. Miers, 1915–1926.

Electro-Technics (see also under Faculty of Technology) :
  R. Beattie, 1912–1938.
  W. Jackson, 1938–1946.
  F. C. Williams, 1946–.

Engineering (see also under Faculty of Technology) :
  O. Reynolds, 1868–1905.
  S. Dunkerley, 1905–1908.
  J. E. Petavel, 1908–1919.
  A. H. Gibson, 1920–1949.

D. R. Hartree (*Engineering Physics*), 1945–1946 (see also under *Mathematics* and *Physics*).

J. L. Matheson, 1950–.

Chemistry (see also under Faculty of Technology) :
E. Frankland, 1851–1857.
H. E. Roscoe, 1857–1886.
C. Schorlemmer (*Organic Chemistry*), 1874–1892.
H. B. Dixon, 1887–1922 (see also under *Metallurgy*).
W. H. Perkin (*Organic Chemistry*), 1892–1912.
A. Lapworth (*Organic Chemistry*), 1913–1935.
R. Robinson (*Organic Chemistry*), 1923–1928.
I. M. Heilbron (*Organic Chemistry*), 1933–1938.
M. Polanyi (*Physical Chemistry*), 1933–1948 (see also under *Political Economy*).
A. R. Todd (*Organic Chemistry*), 1938–1944.
E. L. Hirst (*Organic Chemistry*), 1944–1947.
E. R. H. Jones (*Organic Chemistry*), 1947–.
M. G. Evans (*Physical Chemistry*), 1948–.

Metallurgy :
H. B. Dixon, 1887–1906 (see also *Chemistry*).
H. C. H. Carpenter, 1906–1913.
C. A. Edwards (*Metallurgy and Metallography*), 1914-1920.
F. C. Thompson, 1921–.

Botany :
W. C. Williamson, 1851–1891 (until 1872, his title was *Natural History*, comprising *Vegetable Physiology* and *Botany*, *Animal Physiology* and *Zoology*, and *Geology*).
F. E. Weiss, 1892–1930.
W. H. Lang (*Cryptogamic Botany*), 1909–1940.
J. M. F. Drummond, 1930–1946.
C. W. Wardlaw (*Cryptogamic Botany*), 1940–.
E. Ashby, 1946–1950.
S. C. Harland, 1950–.

Zoology :
W. C. Williamson, 1851–1879.
A. Milnes Marshall, 1879–1893.
S. J. Hickson, 1894–1926.
J. S. Dunkerly, 1926–1931.
H. Graham Cannon, 1931–.
R. Dennell (*Experimental Zoology*), 1948–.

Geology :
W. C. Williamson, 1851–1872.
W. Boyd Dawkins, 1874–1908.
T. H. Holland, 1909–1919.
O. T. Jones, 1919–1930.
W. J. Pugh, 1931–1950.
W. A. Deer, 1950–.

Psychology :
T. H. Pear, 1919–.

Law and Jurisprudence :
R. C. Christie, 1855–1869 (see also *History* and *Political Economy*).
James Bryce, 1870–1875.

Law :
Alfred Hopkinson, 1875–1890 (P–T) and 1898–1913.
J. E. C. Munro (P–T), 1882–1892.
W. A. Copinger (P–T), 1892–1910.
J. S. Seaton (P–T), 1892–1918.
J. L. Brierly, 1920–1923.
R. A. Eastwood (*Law*), 1923–1946, with title *English Law*, 1946–.
F. du P. Oldfield (*Jurisprudence*), 1923–1928.
B. A. Wortley (*Jurisprudence and International Law*), 1946–.
W. Mansfield Cooper (*Industrial and Commercial Law*), 1949–.

Biblical Criticism and Exegesis :
A. S. Peake, 1904–1929.
C. H. Dodd, 1930–1935.
T. W. Manson, 1936–.

Comparative Religion :
T. W. Rhys Davies (P–T), 1904–1915.
J. N. Farquhar (P–T), 1923–1929.
J. Murphy (P–T), 1930–1941.
L. E. Browne (P–T), 1941–1946.
F. H. Smith (*Comparative Religion and Philosophy of Religion*), 1946–1951.

Philosophy of Religion :
W. H. Moberly, 1926–1934.

Anatomy :
M. Watson, 1874–1885.
A. H. Young, 1885–1909, and until 1893 called also professor of *Surgical Pathology*.

G. Elliot Smith, 1909–1919.
J. S. B. Stopford, 1919–1937 (see also *Experimental Neurology*).
F. Wood Jones, 1938–1945.
G. A. G. Mitchell, 1946–.

Experimental Neurology:
J. S. B. Stopford, 1937– (see also *Anatomy*).

Physiology:
W. Smith (P–T), 1873–1875.
A. Gamgee (P–T), 1873–1875.
W. Stirling, 1886–1919.
A. V. Hill, 1920–1923.
H. S. Raper (*Physiology*), 1923–1946; (*Chemical Physiology*), 1946–.
W. Schlapp, 1946–.

Pharmacology, Materia Medica and Therapeutics:
D. J. Leech, 1881–1900.
R. B. Wild, 1901–1927.
A. D. Macdonald, 1935–.
T. H. Oliver (P–T), (*Therapeutics*), 1946–1948 (see also *Clinical Medicine*).

Pharmacy:
H. Brindle, 1946–.

Comparative Pathology and Bacteriology:
A. S. Delépine, 1891–1910.

Public Health:
Arthur Ransome, 1894–1895.

Public Health and Bacteriology:
A. S. Delépine, 1910–1921.

Bacteriology:
W. W. C. Topley, 1922–1927.
H. B. Maitland, 1927–.

Social and Preventive Medicine:
A. Topping, 1947–1950.

Pathology and Pathological Anatomy:
J. Dreschfeld, 1881–1891 (became professor of *Medicine* in 1891 and until 1904 *Pathology* was handled by A. S. Delépine as part of his commitments in *Comparative Pathology*).
J. Lorrain Smith, 1904–1912.

Pathology and Pathological Anatomy—cont.
    A. E. Boycott, 1912–1914.
    H. R. Dean, 1915–1922.
    J. Shaw Dunn, 1922–1931.
    S. L. Baker (*Pathology and Pathological Anatomy*), 1931–1950; (*Osteo-Pathology*),
       1948–.
    A. C. P. Campbell, 1950–.

Medicine :
    W. Roberts (P–T), 1873–1887.
    J. E. Morgan (P–T), 1873–1891.
    J. Ross (P–T), 1887–1892.
    J. Dreschfeld (P–T), 1891–1907.
  From 1908 to 1937, see *Systematic Medicine.*
    F. E. Tylecote (P–T), 1937–1939.
    R. Platt, 1945–.

Clinical Medicine :
    Graham Steell (P–T), 1907–1911.
    J. S. Bury (P–T), 1911–1912.
    E. S. Reynolds (P–T), 1913–1921.
    A. Ramsbottom (P–T), 1921–1937.
    T. H. Oliver (P–T), 1940–1946 (see also *Therapeutics*).

Systematic Medicine :
    G. R. Murray (P–T), 1908–1925.
    F. Craven Moore (P–T), 1925–1929.
    F. E. Tylecote (P–T), 1929–1937 (see also *Medicine*).
    J. C. Bramwell (P–T), 1940–1946 (see also *Cardiology*).

Forensic Medicine :
    J. D. Mann (P–T), 1892–1912.
    W. Sellers (P–T), 1912–1918.

Cardiology :
    J. C. Bramwell (P–T), 1946–.

Surgery :
    G. Southam (P–T), 1873–1876.
    E. Lund (P–T), 1873–1888.
    A. W. Hare, 1888–1892.
    T. Jones, 1892–1900.
  From 1900 to 1934 see *Clinical Surgery* and *Systematic Surgery.*

E. D. Telford (P–T), 1934–1936 (see also *Systematic Surgery*).
J. Morley (P–T), 1936–1946.
A. M. Boyd, 1946–.

Clinical Surgery :
F. A. Southam (P–T), 1900–1910.
W. Thorburn (P–T), 1910–1921.
A. H. Burgess (P–T), 1921–1934.

Systematic Surgery :
G. A. Wright (P–T), 1900–1911.
J. W. Smith (P–T), 1911–1922.
E. D. Telford (P–T), 1922–1934 (title then changed to *Surgery*).

Neurological Surgery :
G. Jefferson (P–T), 1939–.

Orthopædic Surgery :
H. Platt (P–T), 1939–.

Otolaryngology :
V. F. Lambert (P–T), 1947–.

Obstetrics and Gynæcology :
T. Thorburn (P–T), 1876–1885.
C. J. Cullingworth (P–T), 1885–1888.
W. J. Sinclair (P–T), 1888–1912.
W. E. Fothergill (P–T), 1920–1926.
D. Dougal (P–T), 1927–1948.
W. I. C. Morris, 1949–.

Clinical Obstetrics and Gynæcology :
A. Donald (P–T), 1912–1925.
W. Fletcher Shaw (P–T), 1925–1943.

Child Health :
W. F. Gaisford, 1947–.

Psychiatry :
E. W. Anderson, 1949–.

Industrial Health (title changed in 1947 to *Occupational Health*) :
R. E. Lane (P–T), 1945–.

Dental Surgery :
F. C. Wilkinson, 1933–1950.

Prosthetic Dentistry :
 E. Matthews, 1946–.

University Chairs in the Faculty of Technology

Mechanical Engineering :
 J. T. Nicholson, 1905–1913.
 A. B. Field, 1914–1917.
 G. G. Stoney, 1917–1926.
 Dempster Smith, 1926–1939.
 H. Wright Baker, 1939–.

Electrical Engineering :
 A. Schwartz, 1905–1912.
 Miles Walker, 1912–1932.
 J. Hollingworth, 1932–.

Technological Chemistry :
 W. J. Pope, 1905–1908.
 E. Knecht, 1909–1918.
 F. L. Pyman, 1918–1927.
 J. Kenner, 1927–1950.

Textile Technology :
 A. J. Turner, 1919–1923.
 F. P. Slater, 1924–1925.
 W. Myers, 1925.
 W. E. Morton, 1926–.

Non-Professorial Members of Senate in Office between 1905 and 1950

Principals of the Municipal School (later College) of Technology :
 J. H. Reynolds, 1905–1912.
 J. C. Maxwell Garnett, 1912–1920.
 B. Mouat Jones, 1921–1938.
 J. E. Myers, 1938–.

Senior Tutor for Men Students :
 E. Fiddes, 1912–1926 (see also under *History*).

Senior Tutor for Women Students :
 Phoebe A. B. Sheavyn, 1912–1925.

University Librarian :
 Moses Tyson, 1939–.

APPENDIX VIII

NUMBERS OF FULL-TIME MEMBERS OF THE TEACHING STAFF BETWEEN 1900 AND 1949

Compiled by F. P. WALTON, *Assistant Registrar*

Note. (i) The classification is made under the various headings of the returns supplied to the University Grants Committee. These returns were first made for the session 1925–1926 and the figures for the preceding years have therefore been made to approximate as closely as possible to the analysis employed since 1925; between 1900 and 1925, the figures are only given for every third year.

(ii) In each year the figures given under (*a*) are those of the number of full-time teaching staff of departments housed on the main university site or in York Place, those under (*b*) relate to the number of university staff in the Faculty of Technology, established in 1905.

(iii) The figures for Faculties other than Technology include the staff of the Advisory and Research Sections of the Agricultural Department, most of whom appear under the column headed "Others".

Session	Professors	Readers and Independent Lecturers	Lecturers	Assistant Lecturers, Demonstrators and Instructors	Others	Totals
1900–1901	(*a*) 24	—	7	36	—	67
1903–1904	(*a*) 27	2	20	24	—	73
1906–1907	(*a*) 29	3	24	41	—	97 }113
	(*b*) 3	5	2	6	—	16
1909–1910	(*a*) 31	4	29	41	—	105 }136
	(*b*) 3	7	2	19	—	31
1912–1913	(*a*) 35	7	29	38	5	114 }152
	(*b*) 2	9	3	24	—	38

183

Session	Professors	Readers and Independent Lecturers	Lecturers	Assistant Lecturers, Demonstrators and Instructors	Others	Totals	
1915–1916	(a) 36	7	28	40	14	125	167
	(b) 3	7	5	27	—	42	
1918–1919	(a) 38	10	36	26	3	113	165
	(b) 4	8	22	18	—	52	
1921–1922	(a) 41	11	62	45	2	161	222
	(b) 4	7	23	27	—	61	
1925–1926	(a) 38	9	65	45	—	157	219
	(b) 3	9	18	32	—	62	
1926–1927	(a) 37	10	66	46	1	160	228
	(b) 4	7	24	33	—	68	
1927–1928	(a) 36	12	69	47	9	173	240
	(b) 4	7	23	33	—	67	
1928–1929	(a) 34	13	74	48	5	174	243
	(b) 4	6	26	33	—	69	
1929–1930	(a) 34	11	77	52	10	184	253
	(b) 4	7	25	33	—	69	
1930–1931	(a) 36	10	78	52	10	186	258
	(b) 4	6	27	35	—	72	
1931–1932	(a) 36	10	79	55	12	192	264
	(b) 4	6	25	37	—	72	
1932–1933	(a) 36	10	79	55	11	191	267
	(b) 4	6	26	40	—	76	
1933–1934	(a) 38	11	87	52	18	206	281
	(b) 4	5	27	39	—	75	
1934–1935	(a) 37	13	82	59	18	209	288
	(b) 4	6	27	42	—	79	
1935–1936	(a) 38	13	90	53	19	213	292
	(b) 4	5	28	42	—	79	
1936–1937	(a) 38	14	91	54	18	215	293
	(b) 4	6	27	41	—	78	
1937–1938	(a) 39	12	93	50	18	212	290
	(b) 4	7	27	40	—	78	
1938–1939	(a) 39	13	88	48	18	206	288
	(b) 4	7	26	45	—	82	

1939–1947 : PUBLICATION OF RETURNS SUSPENDED DURING THE WAR

The following analysis gives an example of the figures of a sample year in the mid-war period.

Session	*Professors*	*Readers and Independent Lecturers*	*Lecturers*	*Assistant Lecturers, Demonstrators and Instructors*	*Others*	*Totals*
1943–1944	(*a*) 40	17	86	84	10	237 } 320
	(*b*) 4	7	32	40	—	83

RESUMPTION OF RETURNS TO THE UNIVERSITY GRANTS COMMITTEE

1947–1948	(*a*) 51	14	162	136	32	395 } 538
	(*b*) 4	7	64	68	—	143
1948–1949	(*a*) 60	11	172	139	38	420 } 578
	(*b*) 4	7	71	76	—	158
1949–1950	(*a*) 70	22	303	166	83	644 } 808
	(*b*) 4	7	72	81	—	164

Printed in Great Britain by Butler & Tanner Ltd., Frome and London